# THE AGILE

# POCKET GUIDE

## *A Quick Start to* Making Your Business

## Agile Using Scrum and Beyond

## Peter Saddington

**WILEY**

John Wiley & Sons, Inc.

Cover image: © logorilla/iStockphoto
Cover design: Michael J. Freeland

Published by John Wiley & Sons, Inc., Hoboken, New Jersey.
Published simultaneously in Canada.

For general information on our other products and services or for technical support,
please contact our Customer Care Department within the United States at (800)
762-2974, outside the United States at (317) 572-3993 or fax (317) 572-4002.

Wiley publishes in a variety of print and electronic formats and by print-on-demand.
Some material included with standard print versions of this book may not be included
in e-books or in print-on-demand. If this book refers to media such as a CD or DVD
that is not included in the version you purchased, you may download this material at
http://booksupport.wiley.com. For more information about Wiley products, visit
www.wiley.com.

*Library of Congress Cataloging-in-Publication Data:*
Saddington, Peter, 1982-
  The Agile pocket guide : a quick start to making your business agile using Scrum and
beyond / Peter Saddington.
    p. cm.
  Includes index.
  ISBN 978-1-118-43825-1 (pbk.) ISBN 978-1-118-46179-2 (ebk);
ISBN 978-1-118-46179-2 (ebk); ISBN 978-1-118-46177-8 (ebk)
  1. Agile software development. 2. Software engineering. 3. New products.
4. Production management. 5. Teams in the workplace. 6. Workflow. I. Title.
QA76.76.D47S22 2013
005.1—dc23

2012030655

Printed in the United States of America.

10 9 8 7 6 5 4 3 2 1

# *Contents*

*Contents*

# *About the Author*

Peter Saddington is an experienced Business Transformation and Organizational Coach with Action & Influence, Inc., a research and analytics company that focuses on human dynamics and culture in enterprises. In his work as a software development consultant for 15 years, he supported enterprises such as ING DIRECT, Capital One, T-Mobile, Cisco, Yahoo!, J.Crew, InterContinental Hotels Group, Cbeyond, Primedia, the Centers for Disease Control and Prevention, the Department of Defense, the United States Air Force, Blue Cross Blue Shield, Motorola, Samsung, and the United Nations.

Peter holds three masters degrees (in counseling, education, and divinity) and is Certified Scrum Trainer (CST). He has trained hundreds of students in better Agile and Scrum software development methods. He is also the author of *Scrum Pocket Guide—A Quick Start Guide to Agile Software Development*, published in 2010.

An avid writer, Peter is the executive editor of the popular AgileScout.com news blog, which reaches thousands of viewers per day all over the world. He also writes about team optimization and human capital on MyAI.org.

Peter resides in Atlanta, Georgia, with his wife, daughter, and son.

*About the Author*

# *Preface*

"You should write a book."

My boss told me some years ago. At the time I was sending Agile updates to the team every week via e-mail (and I still do this in my consulting and coaching work) about better practices in business transformation, product and software development, and team optimization. These were subjects I knew from experience would help us develop more efficient methods than those we were already using as a team.

But when I began to think about actually writing this book, I was temporarily sidetracked. Was there really a need for yet another book about business transformation and software development, particularly Agile and Scrum software development? (In the 20 years or so since Scrum methodology was first used and called "Scrum" by Jeff Sutherland and Ken Schwaber, a lot has been written on the subject!)

I've read many books by famous authors out there who help the community create better products, increase value across the enterprise, and grow businesses with start-up mentalities. Eric Ries, Scott Belsky, Geoff Smart and Randy Street, and Seth Godin are some of the more popular authors rising today who write about better product development. In terms of Agile software development, Kent Beck, Alistair Cockburn, Ron Jeffries, and Ken Schwaber have been immensely helpful in my years as a trainer and coach in this field—for small and large businesses, nonprofits, and even government agencies.

This guide isn't meant to be part of those great pillars in the Agile and business community; rather, it will offer a unique perspective on what I've personally learned about paving the way to successful Agile cultures within businesses and development teams.

Through my experience of helping transform businesses and helping organizations implement Agile, I've discovered that in the relationship context, a team is more like a Tribe than anything else. It embodies all the positive and negative aspects of a Tribe, and, when encouraged correctly, this Tribe can become not only a high-performance Tribe but also one that can grow in efficiency and influence. It is absolutely crucial that we understand the unique culture and makeup of each Agile Team. I've always said that technology doesn't build great products and software. It's the people that make up a team: how they communicate, collaborate, deal with conflict, and work together successfully that reveals the potential in each individual and unleashes the productivity of teams. You have to know your people. You have to know how to engage and coach correctly and turn each person's potential into value.

*Technology doesn't build great products and software, people do.*

—Peter Saddington

I hope this book helps to clarify and improve the implementation of Agile through organizational change, especially by bringing personal involvement and ownership into the equation. My time will have been well spent if my reflections provide encouragement to any organization willing to embrace best practices in Agile product and software development, and if they can also shed light on the importance of culture within the team. While my personal touch and experience are apparent throughout the book, I do not depict every single applicable theory of Agile; that said, I do cover the main foundational elements of the Scrum framework. I've taken the liberty to format certain aspects of Scrum to best suit general situations. Some will agree; some will disagree. I welcome all feedback and please do e-mail me!

The chapters are not intended to be a hard-core prescription for how to implement Scrum in your organization; these suggestions can provide a framework in which to engage the team so that it can digest the information and own the responsibilities, all at a sufficient pace. Some teams are faster, and some are slower. Some corporate cultures have more red tape while others have less. It's all in how the Agile Leader wants to inform and educate the team about the positive changes necessary to become a high-performance tribe. Every chapter is pretty quick and to the point: each of the first 16 chapters includes a set of three questions meant to elicit the necessary feedback, from either you or your team, for implementing the ideas I discuss, while

Chapters 17 through 24 end with examples of specific scenarios from my own experience as a coach and Agile Leader.

To make sense of this book, you should already be somewhat familiar with Agile principles or have spent some time online reviewing Agile and Scrum.

The quick review of the Agile Manifesto[1] represented by the following list shows priorities at work within the Agile framework:

- Individuals and interactions over processes and tools.
- Working software over comprehensive documentation.
- Customer collaboration over contract negotiation.
- Responding to change over following a plan.

The Agile philosophy simply asks you to work collaboratively as much as possible with your teams and clients to build products with quality, shipping early and often, while learning and relearning along the way.

[1] *Agile Manifesto*. Agilemanifesto.org.

*Preface*

Some principles behind the Agile Manifesto include:

- The highest priority is to satisfy the customer through continuous delivery of valuable software.
- Working software is the primary measure of progress.
- Welcome changing requirements.
- Motivated business people and developers work together throughout the project with face-to-face interactions.
- The team has a commitment to technical excellence at all times.
- At regular intervals, the team reflects on how to become more effective.

You can find more information at www.agilemanifesto.org.

The following list provides a quick summary of Scrum basics:

- Scrum is not an acronym but rather a strategy in the game of rugby for getting an out-of-play ball back into play quickly and efficiently.

- In the Scrum approach, the team works together as a whole to focus on business priorities in a "time box," that is to say, releases composed of many short sprints with an incremental improvement of the software after each deployment.
- Scrum includes three main roles: Product Owners, who set the priorities of the software product; the Team, whose members build the product; and a ScrumMaster or Project Leader, who oversees the process and removes impediments to success.
- Scrum is a transparent process based on self-organizing teams that break the workload down into pieces or iterations.
- Scrum iterative development is a continual process of evaluation, planning, setting requirements, analysis and design, implementation (deployment of code), and testing.

You can find more information, presentations, and white papers on my website at www.agilescout.com. All material is copyrighted by its respective author. For more information on the basic tenants of Scrum, please visit www.scrum.org.

My best wishes to all those out there willing to employ Agile principles. Let me know how things are going on Twitter (@agilescout) or e-mail me at peter@myai.org. I'm always willing to share information and discuss issues.

Best,
Peter Saddington – Mdiv, CST

# *Acknowledgments*

A great many thanks to everyone who has helped me learn better practices in business transformation and Agile product development. This book is dedicated to those who have been with me through years of success and failure. It is also dedicated to my mentors who were willing to teach me, coach me, and give me the chance to provide organizational change and positive improvement to their businesses.

I would also like to thank my parents for always supporting me. You two are truly my heroes!

Thanks to my wife, who lets me reach for my dreams, and to my little girl, who keeps me smiling.

Thanks to John, who has never been impressed with me and has always pushed me to excellence.

# Acknowledgments

# *Introduction*

## Team Tribes: A Story

The business jungle is as vast as it can be dangerous. Many different Tribes, or business units, inhabit the jungle, and they rarely interact with one another unless they are trading goods and services, seeking to expand their influence, or fighting. The landscape of the jungle is littered with once-meaningful artifacts and orphaned documents, as well as the remains of unfinished projects and the ashes of currency and project funds burned away. An overall fear of the unknown marks the well-tread paths that lead to each Tribe. This is not a safe jungle, and if you were to go off the beaten path, you would find the warning markers of imminent danger and the tombs of those who tried to change culture. Members of some departments often visit the shrines that surround the mystical waterfall, where the cadenced flow of the water reminds them of well-instituted processes and procedures that tend to keep the world in balance. Each business Tribe is different, with its own culture and history, and each has its own fears and reservations about change.

A typical business Tribe works very well within its own boundaries and influence. Each business unit contains a leader-diplomat who goes out to work with the other leaders of the different Tribes. The leader-diplomats are usually pillars within their departments and are well equipped with the knowledge of how things are done. They are the keepers of the status quo, and they can exert great influence over others when they see an opportunity to make better use of the Tribe's talents.

You have been selected as the next Leader or Scrum-Master for one of the most reclusive and curious teams in the jungle: the Agile Team. In the recent past, this Tribe has time and time again shown the other members in the business its effectiveness in completing goals. When trading with other teams, leaders in application development see your Agile Team as the most cost-effective Tribe in the land. The leaders of other departments are becoming more aware of the Agile Team and have taken quite an interest in how they may be able to leverage or utilize the often-misunderstood yet awe-inspiring, up-and-coming Tribe. Less and less are the leaders going to the mystical waterfall for guidance; they are now coming to you for help. The time is ripe to establish your team. You are the Leader who will adhere to the principles that make your Agile Team successful. Ready? Go!

Any story about Agile, Scrum, and Team Tribes will include a unique cast of characters who define their

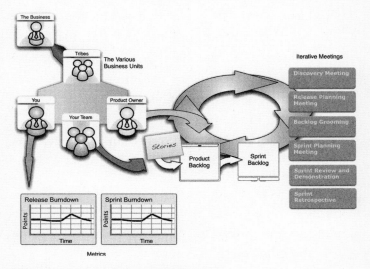

**Figure i.1    The Scrum Process**

*Introduction*

own terms, and who engage with each other as they work through a cycle of various events (i.e., iterative meetings). (See Figure i.1.)

## Characters

Agile Team: Your cross-functional Agile product or software development team.

Leader: The project/program leader, ScrumMaster, or coach for the Agile Team.

Product Owner: The person responsible for defining the requirements and Product Backlog (often as known as "the client"), who prioritizes and grooms user stories for readiness.

Stakeholder(s): Business individual(s) to whom the Product Owner reports.

Tribes: Various business units and stakeholders within the business.

## Definitions

Agile: A framework for delivering products quickly and efficiently.

Cross-Functional Team: A team made up of individuals who can wear many different hats and fulfill many different roles (i.e., a developer doesn't only code, he also does quality assurance and analysis).

Epic: A large requirement or composite user story that needs to be broken down into small segments during software development.

Iteration: A set period of time designated as part of the incremental process of developing and producing the software using an Agile framework (see Sprint and Timebox).

Product Backlog: A list of all user stories for a product.

Release Burndown: Measures the entire backlog of items over the course of the release plan.

Sprint: A set period of time in which to complete a task (see Iteration and Timebox).

Sprint Burndown: Measures the completion of items over the course of a sprint.

Sprint Backlog: A list of user stories for a specific sprint.

*Introduction*

Sprint Review: A demonstration of the product at the end of a sprint.

Theme: A group of common user stories for a sprint or iteration that the team wants to deliver.

Timebox: An Agile software development tool that allows your team to manage a Sprint and determine the appropriate period of time in which to develop features and user stories.

User Stories: Functional units of work (i.e., software requirements to satisfy, such as adding a pull-down menu to a website).

Velocity: A metric for measuring the rate at which teams deliver business value (add up features delivered over an iteration). Often viewed in a Sprint or Release Burndown Chart.

Waterfall: A very defined software development methodology defining *progress* as a steady downward flow that requires completion of a process before a next process can begin.

Your Agile Team will go through several discovery and planning processes before a software product is ready for release. (See Figure i.2.)

*The Agile Pocket Guide*

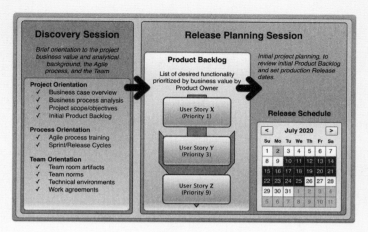

**Figure i.2   Overview of Discovery and Release Planning Process within Scrum**

## Meetings

Discovery Meeting: Initial introduction to a project.

Refactoring Meeting: Review of code and work that needs to be fixed from a previous iteration.

Release Planning Meeting: High-level breakdown of project sprints and delivery dates.

Sprint Planning Meeting: Breaking all stories down into Timeboxed iterations.

Sprint Review Meeting: A time for the team to review and show work completed during a sprint.

Sprint Retrospective Meeting: Review of a previous iteration.

Backlog Grooming Session: Functional breakdown of project items or requirements into developable or actionable units of work.

Sprint cycles, including the Daily Scrum, are crucial to the iterative framework of Agile software development. (See Figure i.3.)

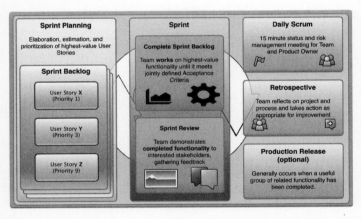

**Figure i.3  Overview of the Sprint Cycle within Scrum**

*The Agile Pocket Guide*

# Chapter 1

# Servant Leadership

Y ou have been chosen to be the next leader of the Agile Team simply because you embody three basic attributes that any successful leader needs: servant leadership, trust-building skills, and an awesome ability to communicate and facilitate. Your ability to lead and coach others springs from your humility and accommodating attitude. You are willing not only to do what it takes to be the best but also to take the low road and serve others through your work. People know they can count on you, and your ability to hold and regain people's trust enables you to build a team of trust, transparency, and accountability. You are a great communicator and protector of the team. Your ability to resolve conflicts among team members as well as business folk allows you to command an audience that trusts your judgment and relies on your ability to protect the team's work from outside influences, filtering only that which is beneficial and helpful to the work at hand. You are an educator in that you coach and teach the business people and product owners how to supply your team with the right amount of information and feedback. You are not haughty, nor are you overbearing. You are the right person for this job.

Your job is to:

- Remove obstacles or resolve dependencies between team members and teams.
- Remind the team of mission/value statements for each project.
- Ensure that the team adheres to the defined rules of Scrum or processes accepted by the team.
- Protect the team and filter nonessential information and meetings.
- Give updates and information regarding enterprise releases or project updates.
- Set the example for the team and for the business.

A wise person once said, "Where there is no vision, the people perish." As the leader you hold the true mission and vision of the business in your hands. Your knowledge of how your team's work directly impacts the overall business is crucial to making sure that anything your team accomplishes falls in line with your business's model for success. Your team will look to you for that direction. They will look to you for example. They will trust your decisions. They will follow your lead.

## Leader Questions

Every chapter in this book ends with a set of three questions you will want to ask your team.

1. Who do we need to meet with or connect with to help with that task?
2. Is there anything we've missed or not considered?
3. What do you need from me, and what can I do to help?

# Chapter 2

# What the Business Wants from You—Managing Requirements

The jungle is perilous, fraught with danger, and always in a state of change. In your jungle, the business comprises many different tribes, teams, or departments. Each of these units within this business has its own personality and history. Even though the business is one major unit, the factions give rise to warring with one another and fighting for the same resources—namely, your Agile Team.

The jungle is not a safe place for even trade. The leaders of each tribe try to work with one another to find a common ground, and they work with you as they give rise to half-baked parchments of work (requirements). The marketing tribe to the sales tribe, the finance tribe to the customer service tribe—all need to utilize your team in order to get what they need done. Unfortunately, they don't always know what "done" is, and they often give you incomplete or nebulous requirements. The tribes have heard that your new Agile Team is taking a new approach to development that is agile, flexible, transparent, and adaptable. How will you communicate to the business that your tribe and Agile practices will knock their socks off? How can you convince them that taking an Agile approach is far better than the mystical waterfall processes and approaches?

So why are Agile requirement processes and change management good for the tribes?

1. Stakeholders and interested parties get to work together to build the right requirements.
2. Stakeholders get constant daily feedback on updates.

3. Stakeholders have control over the scope: they can change requirements and priorities, add new requirements, and modify the product backlog.
4. Stakeholders have control over the schedule (they can fund the project iterations as long as they want).
5. Stakeholders have control over the budget.

The other tribes or business units are excited to hear that they can heavily participate in many aspects of the predevelopment process, but it is your job to remind them that they are responsible for making decisions and providing information and requirements to your team in a timely manner. From here, your team will be able to communicate your time constraints, requirements, questions, and/or needs to the business in a timely manner as well. At the end of the day, the business must own the prioritization of the requirements.

**Leader Questions**

1. Do you currently have a clear understanding of the product landscape or have a product strategy map or product portfolio defined?

*What the Business Wants from You*

**2.** Which features or projects does your business want first?

**3.** Which features or projects will provide the most measurable business value?

# Chapter 3

## Your Agile Team

Your Agile Team is successful because of the unique individuals who make up the team. These members are the heart and soul of your success. Some things to encourage your team with are the continuing autonomy and freedom you give them to do great work. This self-organization is a principle that brings the team together in unity, in that they are generalists and specialists at the same time. The team has the right to take requirements and specifications and build pieces of the total system in the way that they see fit.

There are two ways to approach managing your Agile Team: task-oriented and relation-oriented. Your success as a team Leader hinges on the help you can give to team members as they learn to relate to each other, not just on the help you provide for tasks you assign. The amount of support you give your team and the communication methods you use are just as crucial to your team's success as improving the lack of collaboration and feedback that they probably endure in a non-Agile environment. One of the most important but often forgotten steps is the need to actively listen to your team. As a Leader, you should plan to learn from your team, and one of the best ways to learn is to listen to what they have to say. The best teams are small in size, five to nine cross-functional members work together like a charm!

Teams organize work and tasks among themselves using the following qualities and/or skills:

- Accountability: Team members are held accountable for their work and are reviewed by each team member.
- Teamwork: Team members can work together to utilize their own talents in any project or activity.
- Adaptability: Team members are able to make better decisions based on their own skills and are able to adapt to changes more quickly.

- Collaboration: Team members can circulate knowledge and experience more expediently and make decisions together.
- Communication: Team members who work closely together can communicate and collaborate on work more efficiently.

This culture of empowerment enables team members to look at their responsibilities as more than just a defined role. Each team member can draw from personal experiences, motivations, and passions. With this empowerment comes the ability for each member to have control over how he or she works and to have a purpose of aligning individual aspirations not only with the company goals but also with personal goals and personal growth strategies. One way to elicit this type of information is to sit down individually with each member and ask a few questions. These questions require you to go beyond the call of duty. It takes time and dedication to know your team and determine how individual skills or passions could be matched with business opportunities. To get to the heart of your team culture, you must know your team. (See Chapter 17 for more information on how to understand your team's culture quickly and efficiently.)

## Agile Team Questions

1. What are your roles and responsibilities, and how comfortable are you in them?
2. What works and what does not work with your team?
3. What are other areas that you are interested in helping with or learning about?

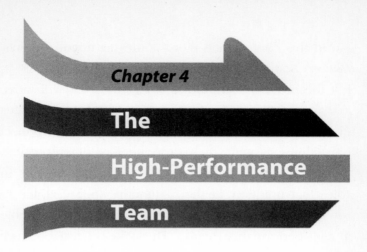

# Chapter 4

# The High-Performance Team

Having a supportive and caring environment to work in may sound simplistic, but whether you're in preschool or a Fortune 500 company, it makes sense. One thing you continually need to communicate to your team is that you and your management care about the relationships within the team. Not only do you care, but you also have high expectations for the team given that the correct structure and guidance are in place. This is also an environment that gives opportunities for meaningful participation in any project and gives recognition to those who do well.

In this context one word comes to mind: *differentiation*. Some people may cringe at the sound of it, but the process it embodies is exactly what will move a team from underperforming (or keeping the status quo) to doing great work and excelling at any project that comes its way. As a proponent of differentiation, I allow the team members to establish themselves in roles that uniquely fit their strengths. (See Chapter 17 for more information on how to build and assemble a high-performance team.) This takes a ton of work from you: you must recognize that there are men and women who keep the lights on and there are those who need to be moved or released back into the jungle. You must be able to spend the time necessary to tap into each team member's potential. People want to flourish and they want to succeed, and to accomplish that, a leader must separate the wheat from the chaff and retain the best talent within a team. Team members will also appreciate your willingness to help them become more productive and valuable to the business, because if you foster an environment of community, collaboration, and caring, you enable members to give feedback on what is working and what is not working, as well as on who is working out and who needs to move on.

High-performance teams are a community. A community environment:

- Breeds group interdependence, which in turn increases the success of individuals as opposed to relying on authoritarian control (top-down management or command-and-control management).
- Enables the team to set goals and solve problems together.
- Continually monitors and assesses work progress.
- Celebrates achievements and rewards individuals.
- Decreases managing overhead by the Leader, thereby enabling the Leader to focus on road-mapping work and giving specialized help as needed.
- Encourages training members as a group, which promotes a higher work ethic and increased productivity.
- Produces measurably great results over time.
- Differentiates roles that people are uniquely fit to fill (see Chapter 17 for more information).
- Coaches the team to give candid feedback and support to other team members.

**15**

*The High-Performance Team*

- Keeps the best talent, moving or removing unproductive members of the team.

A high-performance team is one that embraces the Toyota way of *kaizen*, which means "continuous improvement." Your Agile Team will be one that has members who continually communicate with one another, continually improve themselves, the team, the processes, and the business. Most of all, your team, through its success and transparency, will honor its commitment to the business stakeholders and grow trust between Tribes. Your Agile Team may be ready to move in this direction; if this is the case, task the members to consider their readiness and willingness.

## Leader Questions

1. Do we have the processes and tools in place to build this type of community?
2. Are we physically located in an area that promotes communication and collaboration?
3. Are we meeting regularly enough to go over existing problems, improve existing processes, and be aware of current and future needs?

# Chapter 5

# Everyone around
## the Campfire

Communication is key in the Agile Team. You will want to remove any barriers among team members so that everyone has open lines of communication. The word *campfire* is often used to suggest an open-office environment in which the team can operate so that communication and collaboration are at its most effective levels. This kind of work environment is very unlike that of a cube farm, especially because it does not encourage isolating its members.

You may have to do some heavy lifting to move your team to an open campfire atmosphere. You may find resistance from some very territorial members, and you will very likely find resistance from any who have been around for a long time. We are creatures of habit; but in this case, everyone must be involved, and you must foster the ownership of this initiative with your team. Begin the conversation with your team about how this may happen. Team members may have some great ideas about how to collocate as many parties as possible in one centralized area. Some may not want to move, and I've had more than my fair share of experiences with these types of individuals. Don't worry! They will find out that they've become major blocks to progress, or else they'll find themselves moving on to different positions or companies. W. Edwards Deming, a U.S. statistician and author who taught top management how to improve the quality of products said, that "learning is not compulsory, but neither is survival." These words resonate with most people, and in due time the pragmatic value of moving closer together will be apparent for your entire team. The benefits of an open campfire or open office are as follows:

- All team members are in close proximity to one another; the closer, the better. Facing one another helps, too. (See Figure 5.1.)

**Figure 5.1   Collaborative Common Areas for Team Members**

- All team members are in one centralized area where most of the work is done.
- All team members have access to whiteboards or walls. These walls are used to display charts (information radiators), whiteboard ideas, or brainstorm ideas with sticky notes. (See Figures 5.2 and 5.3.)
- All team members have access to individual privacy areas for "heads-down" work or personal time.

*Everyone around the Campfire*

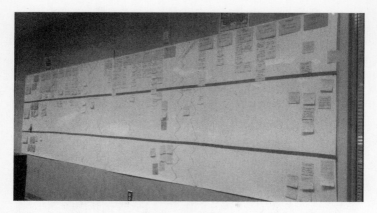

**Figure 5.2    Big Wallboards for Transparency and Team Alignment**

- All team members are encouraged to work with their team to build an optimal work environment that makes sense for them.

Sometimes we have augments or dispersed team members that are not local to the main Agile Team. Offshoring comes to mind as an example. Distributed teams, or teams that are not physically located together, can work together with collocated (local) teams as long as they adhere to the community principles of the high-performance team discussed in Chapter 4. Take your

**20**

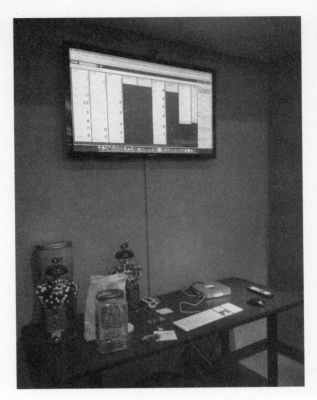

**Figure 5.3   Information Radiator with an Electronic Task Board**

21

*Everyone around the Campfire*

time to figure out which practices work and which do not. If each team member has a mind-set of continual improvement and constant communication, then the Agile Team can eventually determine the most effective practices within your development environment.

There are also communication software packages available for purchase that allow dispersed teams to communicate with one another. Again, take your time figuring out what works best within your organization and team. Remember, software platforms do not replace methodologies and good practices and/or processes. Software shouldn't be the first go-to response for any issue before fully examining the methods and processes in place. The questions for your team are meant to build up unity and cohesiveness toward this open-office goal. The more support you have from the people doing the hard labor, the more this activity of moving around desks or breaking down cubicle walls will be seen as a team project.

Go to www.agilescout.com/best-agile-tools to find a list of more than 100 collaborative and Agile and Scrum tools to use for your team.

## Agile Team Questions

1. What are the potential benefits and drawbacks of having an open office?

2. What would be the most effective way of moving ourselves to an open-office environment?

3. What are the roadblocks that must be discussed and overcome to enable us to have an open office?

# Chapter 6

## Daily Stand-Up,
## or Daily Scrum

Your Agile Team is more effective than any other Tribe out in the jungle because your team members constantly communicate with one another. One of the best ways to encourage this is through a Daily Stand-Up, or Daily Scrum. This is a daily morning meeting that facilitates team communication, fosters teamwork, discloses details of the project work, and highlights items for review, action, or execution. Every member of the project is invited, and every member of the Agile Team must participate; those who are outside of the core team should be silent participants. This stand-up meeting fosters shared accountability; it allows all members to be in tune with the challenges of the day and respond quickly to those challenges. This meeting is conducted standing up for a reason: it shouldn't last for more than 15 to 20 minutes. (See Figure 6.1.) Sometimes the team will go into more detailed discussion during this time; table it, and take it offline for further discussion after the meeting. Remember that the team members aren't

**Figure 6.1   A Team Conducting a Daily Scrum**

addressing you with a status update; rather, they are addressing the team about their work and their issues. There is no hierarchy in this meeting; no single person needs to lead it every day.

Each member of the Agile Team is expected to answer three questions as part of the Daily Scrum (see Figure 6.2):

1. What did I do (and what did I complete) yesterday?
2. What am I planning to do (and committing to complete) today?
3. What impediments do I have that may block my success today?

Your leadership is crucial to the success of this daily meeting, even when other team members take turns facilitating it. You set the example for the rest of the team and show them that they can depend on you to remove impediments and grease the wheels of productivity. Your example should reveal the importance of this daily stand-up, and you should ask the right questions to elicit good communication and collaboration within

**27**

*Daily Stand-Up, or Daily Scrum*

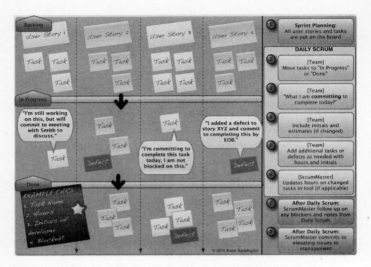

**Figure 6.2   A Storyboard Illustrating Tasks Discussed during a Daily Scrum**

the team. The specificity of your questions will reaffirm to the team that they are committing to work every day. Noncommittal behavior can easily arise from bland and vague updates. Remember that the purpose of this meeting is to align the team and commit to completing certain tasks on that day.

## Agile Team Questions

1. When is the best time to have this meeting?
2. Who is designated to lead the meeting and be responsible on different days?
3. What should be the core hours in which team members are available to collaborate with one another?

# Chapter 7

# Introducing the
# Product Owner,
# or Value Driver

The functions of Tribes vary: there is always a ton of work to be done ranging from analysis and research to building, hunting, and even warring. Because so many top priorities and competing interests exist in many different areas of business, we assign a Product Owner, or Value Driver, to a special leading role within the business. I often call these individuals *Value Drivers* because they fully and uniquely understand the priorities of different business units (and how the Agile

Team must address them); they know where the highest value is at any given moment because they continually make decisions to ensure that the features or functions with the biggest benefit to the business receive primary consideration.

Product Owners (Value Drivers) work directly with Agile Teams, helping the members prioritize their workload, and also serve as intermediaries between the users and the Agile Teams. What needs to be built now? The Product Owners know, because they define project scopes and requirements. What needs to be built next? Product Owners know that too, because they prioritize and order the work. What does the team need to prepare for? Product Owners are already one step ahead in that they constantly groom the next set of requirements and priorities for their respective teams to consume. Product Owners also work directly with the stakeholders—those who give the Product Owner strategy. This is a one-person job, not a role to be filled by a group. While other individuals may have a say in the priority or value of a feature or function, they must go through the Product Owner, and the Product Owner makes the changes. The Product Owner's primary concern is the content of the product and the specifics entailed, while your Agile Team's expertise provides the implementation and development of the product.

So, to begin moving toward facilitating the Scrum framework, your team must have a clearly defined Product Owner. This single person must possess the following characteristics:

- Intimate knowledge about priorities—an understanding of what the Agile Team needs to build or to do next.
- A high level of engagement with the Agile Team and a reasonable availability to help refine requirements.
- The ability to serve as a direct link between you and the stakeholders.
- Enough respect and empowerment to make value and priority decisions that the business needs.
- The ability to serve as the primary funnel and filter through which other conflicting priorities are settled.

The Product Owner (Value Driver) is a VIP because that single person knows the explicit and implicit value of the programs and projects that need to get done. The Product Owner gives the team unambiguous direction and allows the team to focus on that direction without having to worry about conflicting business priorities. The Product Owner is also the first line of business engagement for the Agile Team, providing support proactively and continuously to the team as a result of constant communication with customers and stakeholders about the details and priority of the product. The Product Owner is also available to each member

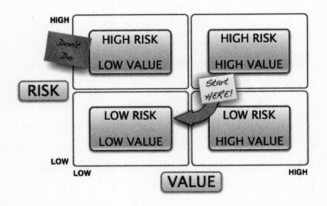

**Figure 7.1  A Value Matrix Determining Workflow Priority**

of the team and is thus invaluable, ensuring that team members have the information they need to build the best product.

Remember, the Product Owner should prioritize the work by value. A value matrix can help your Product Owner determine what features should be built first. (See Figure 7.1.) Start with the highest value features!

## Agile Team Questions

1. **1.** Does your Product Owner have the qualifications necessary?
2. **2.** Does your Product Owner have the visibility and the empowerment to make priority decisions?
3. **3.** Does your Product Owner have the availability and engagement to provide the right guidance and course direction for the team?

*Introducing the Product Owner, or Value Driver*

# Chapter 8

## Discoveries from the Product Backlog

The Product Backlog is a list of all the tasks the Agile Team will work on for a particular project. After giving the orders of work and the priority of those orders, a Product Owner will walk to the Product Backlog and post them. All team members go to the Product Backlog for their work orders. This backlog is centrally located so that no one has an excuse for not knowing what to do, and it is ever-growing and changing for each project. (The Product Backlog is never complete.) At the beginning of a project, the Product Owner meets with the Agile Team and you, its Leader, to discuss the overall project and the highest-level details of what needs to be built.

Some teams have called this initial meeting a discovery meeting. Discovery meetings are usually pretty short, and the team doesn't spend too much time at them, although they may cover everything from the features and functions that will be built out for the project.

**Figure 8.1    A Packed Product Backlog Needing to be Completed for a Release**

One way to start building out the Product Backlog is to fill it up with as many requirements as a certain project may demand (see Figure 8.1) and then break them out into different *user stories*, or tasks (more on this in Chapter 9). As this list grows, you'll probably want to add some grouping mechanisms to organize the work. The use of *tags*, or group names, is a good way to start.

The Product Owner, who also owns the Product Backlog, must:

- Prioritize the backlog, placing the most important functionality at the top and the least at the bottom, according to business value.

- Be ready to consult and give guidance on any questions the team has about the product.

- Allow for any technical task to be inserted as a corollary to some of the tasks on the Product Backlog.

- Be able to give more detail to the higher priority items and articulate the value associated with the top items on the Product Backlog.

*Discoveries from the Product Backlog*

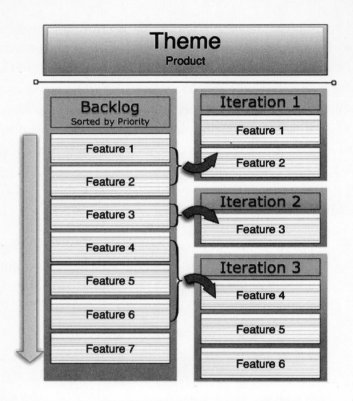

**Figure 8.2 A Backlog Prioritized Top to Bottom and Divided into Iterations**

After the Product Backlog has been filled up with high-level stories, or functional units of work, the team is ready to estimate and task out work for a sprint. (See Figure 8.2.) Your Scrum team is getting ready to build something fantastic. Get ready—the work is about to begin!

## Agile Team Questions

1. Has your Product Owner spent just enough time building out the requirements or foreseeable tasks to the Product Backlog?

2. Does your team have enough information from the Product Owner to begin work immediately?

3. Do you know of any impediments, constraints, or dependencies that the team needs to be advised of?

# Chapter 9

## The Sprint Backlog
## and Release Planning

After the Product Owner has identified and prioritized all of the work items, the Agile Team then goes off to estimate the workload of the highest-priority items into a Sprint Backlog. The Sprint Backlog is the list of requirements or tasks that will be completed during a sprint, or set period of time. All of the items in the Sprint Backlog must be distilled enough for a team member to work on. Ideally these items will be broken out and sufficiently defined so that a team member can finish a piece of work within a day.

Everything in the jungle has a soul and a story—even project work. Since the Product Backlog holds all the items and functionality that needs to be built into a product, the Agile Team breaks down the work into user stories in a *backlog grooming session*. A backlog grooming session can take place at the beginning of a project, but should also continue constantly through the sprint cycle. This meeting is the meat and potatoes of the preliminary tasks that need to be done before work begins. The team members take as long as necessary to put flesh on the bare-bones tasks (called a grooming session). (Figure 9.1 shows tasks broken down by theme.) This can take a couple hours while the entire team works in coordination to put all of the stories together to fit in the first sprint. (Sometimes a grooming session is combined with sprint planning, as described in Chapter 10.) This first sprint is a Timeboxed iteration. As teams progress and mature, I recommend that Product Owners and Agile Teams constantly take time out of a current sprint to groom the backlog and stories in preparation for the next sprint. This makes sprint planning shorter and allows the work to go more smoothly, and it has the potential to remove issues before the next sprint begins.

Many Agile Teams have found that two- or four-week Timebox iteration works very well in the

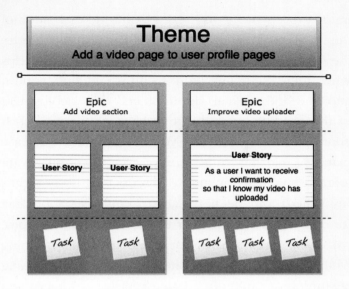

**Figure 9.1    A Theme Broken Down to the Task Level**

beginning. Sometimes this Timeboxed sprint can move to one week! What can be necessary with larger projects, but is not always so for smaller projects, is a *release planning meeting*. Simply put, this meeting between the Product Owner and the team is to discuss, from a high-level view, the final deliverables, the team's initial capacity for work, and a high-level estimation of the approximate work that will be needed to complete the entire project. The release planning meeting helps when there is enough work to fill up multiple sprints, and the incremental development and deployment of the product needs to be tracked and managed. If your team determines that you need to have a release planning meeting for a larger project, then you'll want to make sure that you meet to discuss how many sprints (estimated) will be necessary to complete a product for deployment. Remember to record all the decisions, risks, and assumptions that come with the planning of the releases. The outcome of the release planning meeting is to build out a framework (or roadmap) and initial estimate for the delivery of the product. (See Figure 9.2.) This plan can and will be revised and changed as the project moves along.

User stories are the backbone of your work. The stories:

- Must be posted in a highly visible area for all to see.
- Must be updated daily.
- Must be as descriptive as possible.

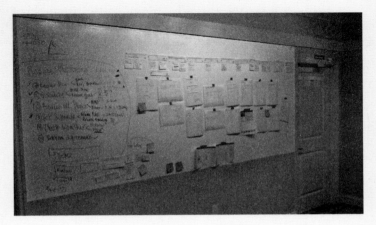

**Figure 9.2  A Release Planning Roadmap with features at the Top, and UI designs and stories below**

- Must be evaluated and estimated for work (more on this in Chapter 10).
- Must be estimated by the team and maintained by you.
- Must be sized correctly to fit in a sprint (more on this in Chapter 11).
- Must come from the Product Backlog.
- Can be added to, removed, or changed, but only by the team.

**47**

*The Sprint Backlog and Release Planning*

The Sprint Backlog can be maintained in several different ways. Remember, the Sprint Backlog is the list of items to be worked on for the time-boxed iteration. Most often, Agile Teams have found that creating a wall that tracks every user story has been successful. It is absolutely imperative that the team and you maintain the items in the Sprint Backlog, as your team will be committing to the completion of the tasks as they are broken down into sprints or iterations.

## Leader Questions

1. Where can the user stories be located centrally for the Agile Team to discuss? Note: You can also use software to track your stories, but many teams have found that a physical wall has been of greatest value (more on this in Chapter 13).

2. Does each project require a release planning meeting?

3. Has everyone on the team participated in the meetings and understood the planned approach to the release of the product?

# Chapter 10

## Sprint Planning Meeting

The Product Owner and you are now ready to set out the schedule of work for the upcoming iterations. The sprint planning meeting is the perfect place to start setting the pace for work. Remember, the team has a good grasp on the vision and purpose of the project, and you are now ready to commit to stories and the work at hand. Now, the Product Owner, you, the entire team, and any other interested members of the business work together to understand how many user stories they can to commit to completing within a given sprint. These sprints hold a certain point value, as we discuss in Chapter 11. At this point the team answers the questions, "What needs to be built first, and can we commit to completing it?" (See Figure 10.1.) These user stories are generally locked in place and committed to by the team. The Product Owner can change some stories and requirements as long as the team commits to completing them or you help the Product Owner understand that some features may be added to the sprint, which may mean that other features will be removed. We then estimate the work as detailed in Chapter 11. It's "go" time. Let's get started.

Note: Many Agile coaches do not have a backlog grooming session prior to a first sprint for a new Agile Team as depicted in Chapter 9. That is absolutely fine! I have found that it is wise to allow the team to learn the process and get a good grasp on breaking requirements into user stories, tasking, estimating, and aligning themselves to a goal. As teams mature, your teams will fly through a sprint planning meeting because you've been grooming the backlog with the Product Owner throughout the week in preparation for the sprint planning meeting.

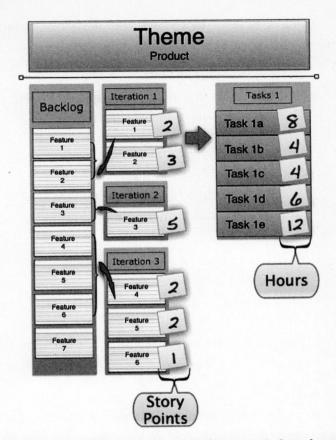

**Figure 10.1  Sizing Stories with Story Points into Tasks with Task Hours**

*Sprint Planning Meeting*

The action items that result from a sprint planning meeting include identification of:

- The sprint goal or theme.
- All items of value that the team intends to deliver.
- The highest-priority value items first.
- The tasks needed to complete each story.
- An agreement process to evaluate any story additions/removals from the sprint.
- How much buffer should be included in the work (e.g., meetings, other responsibilities, ad hoc changes, etc.).
- The commitment by the team to complete all of the assigned stories on time.
- The estimates of the user stories and tasks (more in Chapter 11).
- The Timeboxed length of the sprint (determined initially; from then on it should be a standard amount of time).

From the outpourings of this meeting come a Sprint Plan, or a measurable way to determine the success of the project as well as to ensure that everything committed to in the Sprint Backlog reflects the product or project value. The success of the sprint will later be assessed during a retrospective meeting (covered in Chapter 15).

## Leader Questions

1. Has everyone, especially the Product Owner, participated in the meeting?
2. Has the entire team committed to a plan that is realistic and achievable?
3. Has the Product Owner given the team the most up-to-date information and features as well as an organized and well-understood list of priorities?

## Chapter 11

# User Stories

# and Estimation

Each and every Tribe and business pass down stories from generation to generation. These stories tell of past projects and teachings that the Tribe has learned and grown from. The best of these stories are the ones rich with content, detailed in their specifics and complete in their telling.

Each endeavor for the Tribe is a conglomeration of stories; the more depth these stories have, the easier they are to know, understand, and apply to the project. In total, the stories need to be analyzed and understood by the Agile Team. What comes out of user story writing is the desired functionality of each unit of work for the project. These user stories are often written on index cards or sticky notes. During backlog grooming or sprint planning, the team members will assign themselves stories and commit to the work. Their signature on each user story commits them to the completion of the work. (See Figure 11.1.)

**Figure 11.1   Team Members Assigning Stories and Committing to Work**

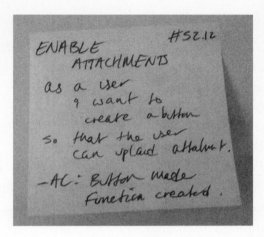

**Figure 11.2   A Story Card Written on a Sticky Note**

Each user story created around a particular feature or functionality always follows the laws of the land in user story creation. (See Figure 11.2.)

- As a <user> I want to <function> so that I can <business value>.
- Acceptance Criteria (AC): <Steps necessary for this story to succeed or be completed>.
- Notes: <Any additional information pertinent for the developer>.
- Priority: <If you have a priority scheme>.
- Effort: <Unit of effort to complete story>.

*User Stories and Estimation*

Here is an example of a story:

*As a <customer> I want to <build a drop-down box on my website> so that <I can easily see a selection of inventory that I can buy>.*

The story's AC includes these five points:

**1.** Drop-down box needs to be gray.

**2.** Drop-down box needs to be 30 pixels in length.

**3.** When clicked, drop-down box must show five items in the beginning with the rest below through a scrollbar.

**4.** Items in the drop-down box must be in alphabetical order.

**5.** Items must also be sorted by size.

Notes: This drop-down box must also include new products we are adding to our inventory in one week. This box is custom created for a top-dollar client.

Priority: 1

Effort: 4

Backlog grooming sessions or sprint planning meetings are also the place where each user story is estimated for level of effort. This is a measurement of complexity of work, not the specific time to complete it. Since we all know we're terrible at estimation, how do we do this?

In estimating stories and work, remember to make sure to:

- Use relative units (e.g., A is half as hard as B).
- Take into account team member skill level, domain knowledge, external interruptions, and unexpected technical issues.
- Solicit group input on the estimations.
- Have everyone estimate in the same units and agree what "done" means.
- Do not estimate when your team is unsure about the specifics of the project.
- Create reference stories that the team can use as a template (or templates) for estimation.
- Be realistic.

There are certain ways of estimating stories. Often teams have found the use of doubles as a great way to estimate (e.g., 1, 2, 4, 8) or the Fibonacci sequence (e.g., 1, 2, 3, 5, 8). With many Agile Teams, any type of estimation of an "8" is considered an "epic" and needs to be broken down into smaller pieces that can be estimated as a 1, 2, 3, 4, or 5 depending on chosen estimation method. These points end up being the velocity that you will use to measure the total amount of work or capacity your team can handle in any given iteration. These points need to take into account external interruptions, technical surprises, team member skill level, domain knowledge, and other factors. Over time, this velocity will need to be stable to accurately measure the team's capacity. The most-used graph for this is a Burndown Chart, which graphs total velocity points over iteration time (more on that in Chapter 13).

The quickest way to estimate user stories is through affinity estimation. (See Figure 11.3.)

Affinity estimation is far better than static guessing of complexity. We are far better at comparing than static estimation, so we make use of our natural gift of comparison to get estimates quickly.

- Put number buckets up on a wall using sticky notes: 1, 2, 3, 5, 8, 13 (Fibonacci). Smallest and least complex user stories on the left, and largest and most complex on the right.

**Figure 11.3    A Team Doing Affinity Estimation**

- The team discusses stories to make sense of them.
- Utilize a baseline story (for a first Sprint), often this is the easiest user story for the team to complete.
- Without conversation, the entire team takes turns moving stories under each numerical bucket as to how complex that story is to complete, also comparing each story to previous stories. (See Figure 11.4.)

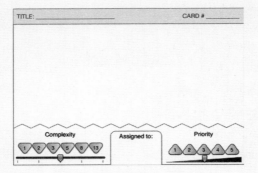

**Figure 11.4   A Story Card Template**

- Anyone can move any story position.
- As activity subsides, collaborate, refine, and then prioritize.
- Task out the prioritized stories and commit!

Planning Poker is another way of estimating stories. You can pick up a deck of Planning Poker cards at http://store.mountaingoatsoftware.com/. Essentially the game plays as follows:

- Each developer has a set of planning cards.
- As each story is brought to the group, all developers flip over an estimation card for the total work to complete the story.

- If all of the estimates are similar, then that is the assigned value.
- If there is a discrepancy between developers' estimates, then a conversation ensues as to why and what the more accurate estimate is.

## Agile Team Questions

1. Who can be responsible to lead the sprint planning or grooming and continue to communicate and uphold the standards of user story creation?
2. What type of estimation point system should we employ?
3. What should be the criteria for complexity when estimating?

Here are some suggestions from authorities in the business about ways to create a good user story:

## Ron Jeffries's 3 Cs[1]

1. Card—each user story is represented by a card or token.
- Conversation—the conversation around that requirement and user story is the most important.

[1]Ron Jeffries. "Essential XP: Card, Conversation, Confirmation." Xprogramming.com/articles/expcardconversationconfirmation/.

- Confirmation—confirmation of understanding (and confirmation of acceptance criteria) ensure that the user story will be completed according to specifications.

## Bill Wake's INVEST Model[2] regarding what a story card should be:

- Independent—each user story should be able to be completed independently, without dependence on another user story.
- Negotiable—each user story should be negotiable around priority, value, and specific requirements necessary for completion.
- Valuable—each user story should have an explicit value to the business.
- Estimable—each user story should be broken down enough to be estimated.
- Small—each user story should be as small as possible so a team can consume and complete user stories quickly.

[2]Bill Wake, "INVEST in Good Stories and SMART Tasks," http://xp123.com/articles/invest-in-good-stories-and-smart-tasks/.

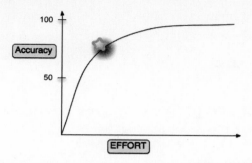

**Figure 11.5   Balancing Accuracy and Effort**

- Testable—each user story must be able to go through all testing requirements and procedures.

Whatever story method you use, or whatever advice you take, remember to not spend excess time estimating! (See Figure 11.5.) Spend just enough time so that you get the right balance of accuracy for amount of effort.

# Chapter 12

# Timeboxed Sprints

# (Iterations) and the

# Meaning of *Done*

Your Agile Team wants to be as productive as possible, but not only that—your team wants to optimize efficiency, increase predictability, and reduce risk. The various other business units are vying for your attention and resources at this moment, and the leaders from those Tribes want to see results as soon as possible. They have almost stopped going to the mystical waterfall and the processes that it instills in people. They are waiting on you to report back to them that work can be done faster than a 9–12 month plan. You have your marching orders. You have a project plan. Now it's time to break those out into logical time units where you can complete working product. Figure 12.1 shows a step toward the goal: product release.

When you have spent time estimating the tasks and features, gather your team and all members working on the particular project. It is now time for them to help you commit to a certain amount of work within a given

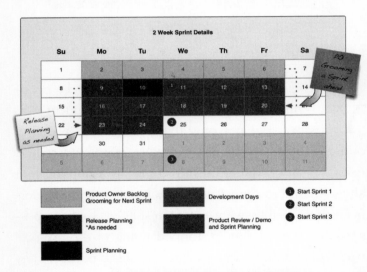

**Figure 12.1    A Release and Sprint Calendar**

*The Agile Pocket Guide*

time frame, and now is the time when using an online Agile tool can help.

Timeboxed sprints need to have the following guidelines:

- The sprint goal is established and well understood throughout the team.
- All sprints are four weeks or fewer. (Many teams have found that they can successfully push product out even in a week!)
- All sprints must end on time.
- All sprints must have a team that is neither interrupted nor controlled by other stakeholders or other business tribes.
- All sprints will complete with almost everything they have committed to. (As your team becomes more accurate, they will be able to complete 100 percent of their features nearly 100 percent of the time.)
- Sprints can be canceled, but only by the Product Owner and/or you, and if there are business reasons for doing so. (Most likely this will not be necessary due to the short length of time the iterations take up.)

**69**

*Timeboxed Sprints and the Meaning of* **Done**

- The shorter your Timeboxed sprints are, the shorter your estimates will be for tasks.

Your Agile Team enjoys the ability to have a lot of wins weekly. This has completely improved your team's culture and attitude at work. This boost in morale is a welcome addition to your team's working environment. Tread carefully here, though; many teams can lack maturity and experience working under these guidelines. That's okay—it is a learning process! When work doesn't get done within a Timeboxed sprint due to overcommitting or underestimating, it is time to gather the team and reflect on how things may be improved. It may mean that the sprints need to be a different length, such as three weeks instead of two. Or it may mean that they need to split the bigger user stories down into smaller user stories. Or, it may mean that the team needs to reflect on how they develop, test, or deploy their code. Take the time necessary to define areas of improvement; these conversations with your team will bring them back up to speed and not keep them in a death-spiral of despair. Be a leader and energize them to work smarter together. Your attitude here is crucial to the success of achieving consistent sprints.

*The Agile Pocket Guide*

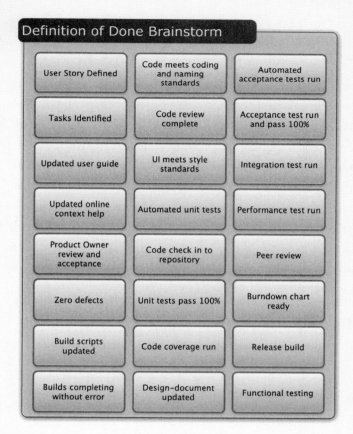

**Figure 12.2  A Brainstorming Session Defining**
***Done***

*Timeboxed Sprints and the Meaning of* Done

One of the major definitions your team has to understand is the meaning of *done*. Business stakeholders, developers, quality assurance personnel, business analysts, and others may assert that *done* means something completely different than it does to others. Regardless of how many definitions are out there, your team must establish a definition of *done* that the Product Owner and team understand clearly. As the Product Owner is clearly the client, his definition of *done* is king. As your team sets out to complete the sprint goal, remember to clearly define what *done* is for your Product Owner. Does it include all requirements, testing, documentation, security, and integration? Or is it something simpler? Define it! (See Figure 12.2.)

### Agile Team Questions

1. What is the best Timeboxed sprint length that your team should employ?
2. What is your team's definition of *done*?
3. What is the defined functionality of a completed iteration?

## Chapter 13

# Tracking Flow and
# Information Radiators

You now have a backlog full of work items, user
stories that have been broken out into sprints, and
a plan to get all of the features done within a certain
time frame. Your team is ready to go. All you need now
is a way to track progress through the sprints. What
you need now is a highly visible area in which you can
build your swim lanes of progress.

Your Agile Team's backlog has all the user stories,
possibly hung on a wall somewhere. How do you track
when the user stories get worked on? A simple process
could be to start with three different swim lanes up

on a wall: *backlog*, *working*, and *done*. Let's say a team member begins work on a user story; she moves it to the working section, and when she is complete, she moves it to the done swim lane. This simple flow is a great starting point for your team. Each team is different, and some enjoy breaking out swim lanes into very specific buckets. See what works best for your team. The charts discussed in this chapter, which can also be called information radiators, provide examples of what other Agile Teams have done to track progress and flow. (See Figures 13.1 and 13.2.)

You have a great idea—two great ideas, in fact. They're called a Burndown Chart and a Release Burndown Chart. These charts enable your team to track daily progress as it is completed. The $x$-axis of the Burndown Chart is your sprint length (in workdays) and the $y$-axis is total number of user story points to be completed during the sprint. For a Release Burndown Chart, the $x$-axis is the total number of sprints and the $y$-axis is the total number of user story points for the entire project. Both of these charts have a line that shows the predicted completion of user stories over time. These are very simple ways for you to track the

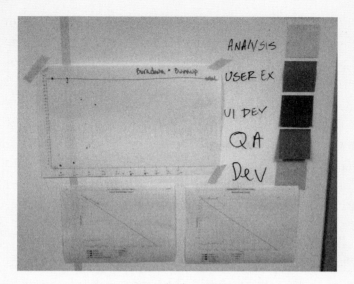

**Figure 13.1 Burndown Charts Make Useful Information Radiators**

progress of the work being done by your team, and they give your team a simplistic view forecasting when the work will be complete.

What happens when work is added midstream or scope is increased? What you will see is a spike in the chart! A regular Burndown Chart won't show you the details if issues arise. Another chart your team likes to

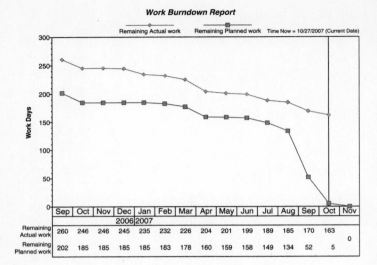

**Figure 13.2    A Burndown Chart Tracking Workdays over Months**

use is a Burnup Chart. This chart is updated daily and shows the total work over the period of time; it also includes a line at the top to show whether additional work has been added or removed. When there are changes to the number of user stories within a sprint or iteration, it is recorded in this chart. Personally, I think a Burnup Chart has more value to the team. It allows the team to see how scope changes can affect timing and whether they are able to adapt to changes on the fly. As user stories are completed, the line goes up toward the total number of story points.

Here are some points to consider when using Burndown or Burnup Charts.

- Charts are simply conversation starters; they should reinforce the need to discuss any deviations or notable changes in work through a sprint or release.

- Charts need to use the team's velocity as a gauge for workload. Do not track hours over time, as that isn't very agile! Estimation points or story points created during the sprint planning meetings are best used. In due time, the team should be able to get to a consistent number or average number of points per sprint.

- Charts allow you to measure the rate of delivering working software to your stakeholders. This velocity should be your main metric in determining work capacity and value.

**77**

*Tracking Flow and Information Radiators*

Tracking the flow and the progress of your team's work is crucial for transparency to both the team and the business. These charts, or information radiators, allow disclosure to be part of the team culture as well as the business culture. Ideally, the charts will allow the team to develop in time a predictable pattern of work and stabilize as the team learns what works and what doesn't. Remember to update all flows and charts daily. Even have your Daily Scrum in front of the information radiators to allow your team to speak to specific user stories or tasks.

## Agile Team Questions

   **1.** Where is the best place to put these information radiators in your office?
   **2.** What trends does your team see over time?
   **3.** Over time, how much work can your team handle within a sprint?

# Chapter 14

# Demonstration

# of the Product

The Tribe is getting excited about putting structure into place where there was none previously. It is apparent that after each sprint there needs to be a demonstration or review of the product so that the Product Owner and business can see the positive output of the Agile Team. This is a great opportunity to get some early feedback from the Product Owner about what is working and acceptable in the product and what isn't. This feedback can help the team during the next sprints to determine what needs to change from the previous sprint. The demonstration of the product needs to showcase a fully functional piece of the product that the team considers reviewable and acceptable by the Product Owner. In software-related environments, the demonstration proves that functionality is potentially shippable, or ready to be put into production. While the demo may be in a development or quality-assurance environment and all functionality may not be accessible, the software needs to be demonstrated as much as the capabilities of the environment allow.

During this demo, you'll want to make sure that the Product Owner is in the driver's seat. You may feel that a developer should show off all of the features, but through experience you'll find that the software sometimes acts differently and may behave in odd ways when someone other than a developer drives. You'll want to make sure that you navigate the meeting so that unnecessary distractions won't stall the completion of the demo. People participating in the demo may have great ideas, but if they aren't part of the agreed-upon features, then take notes and document the comments.

Demos and reviews are crucial because they:

- Happen after every sprint.
- Show working valuable product or tested software.

*The Agile Pocket Guide*

- Enable feedback from the stakeholders and Product Owner to be given to the Agile Team.
- Allow the business the opportunity to sign off on the product (acceptance).

A demo is a time for your Agile Team to shine (See Figure 14.1). Let the team share the features and give context around what the product is if the Product Owner has any questions or needs clarity. Quite possibly, you could demonstrate every user story. Let

**Figure 14.1   A Team Demonstrating Features during a Sprint Review Meeting**

*Demonstration of the Product*

the enjoyment for what has been built come from the inside of the team, not you. Allow the team to revel in this opportunity to show what they have been working so very hard to complete—and on time! This should be an exciting event; let that excitement continue to grow and confidence be built as your team accumulates more and more successful sprints.

The primary goal for your team will be the delivery of the product on time and within user story specifications. This focus allows the team to rally around a definitive goal, and the Product Owner will begin to get more and more involved during the process.

**Leader Questions**

1. Are all of the necessary attendees available for the demo?
2. What is the best way to promote the announcement of the product to the other business units (e.g., an e-mail announcement)?
3. What ways can you reward successfully completed, tested, and working products or software?

Note: I've found that a couple of problems often come up when first instilling a process to demo a product. Regardless, you should always strive to have a demonstration of the product because it can be the single best point during a sprint where hard work is acknowledged and rewarded and the necessary feedback from the stakeholders is documented.

Here are three main issues that might arise when having a product demo:

1. *Functionality cannot always be demonstrated.* Still have a demo. You can use this time to demonstrate nontangible functionality, wireframes, and design compositions, even architecture. Use this opportunity to get feedback from the Product Owner.

2. *Developers do not have the time to do a demonstration.* Allow your team to build in demo time during each sprint or remove a user story or two so that time can be allotted for demos.

3. *Stakeholders and the Product Owner do not attend the demo.* Try scheduling a standing meeting that allows consistency for all parties to attend at the same time and same day for every iteration demo.

**83**

***Demonstration of the Product***

# Chapter 15

# The Retrospective

Team members can be brutally honest. Their honesty needs an outlet. Team members can also be hesitant to share. Their input is valuable, and we need it. A retrospective meeting is a perfect place to enable your entire team to talk about the latest sprint. It is a moment for the team to take a breath and reflect, to find things that worked well, things that needed improvement, and areas of opportunity to improve for the next sprint (Figure 15.1). Everyone must participate and answer the questions on the agenda.

Often the retrospective can be put on the back burner and ignored at the end of a sprint. Do not fail to have a retrospective. Put in a user story card during the

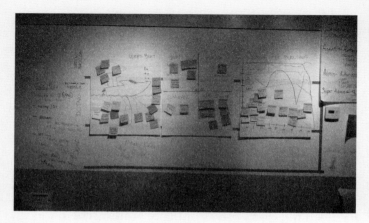

**Figure 15.1 Three Retrospective Workshop Exercises**

iteration to set out time for this meeting if you have to. This retrospective allows your team members to build confidence in one another, inspect the process, adapt, and give you, their Leader, an opportunity to motivate the team and receive feedback. (See Figure 15.2.)

The attributes of the retrospective meeting include the following:

- It happens after every sprint.
- It includes the entire Team and the Product Owner.

**Figure 15.2 The Leader Motivates the Team during a Retrospective**

- It is a safe haven for feedback of any kind (as long as it's tactful and constructive).
- It needs the participation of every single person.
- It needs a good facilitator who can stay out of the conversation and maintain the flow of ideas and thoughts.
- It can be a place where other activities are included. Mix it up!

Some Agile Teams have found that appreciating other people and giving the good news first is a great

*The Retrospective*

way to put your team in a positive frame of mind. This sets them up to take better advantage of opportunities for improvement. Again, honesty is paramount. Your team's ability to improve and see continued success is marked by its members' willingness to critique and challenge one another. Focusing on solutions rather than just the problems can help your Agile Team think as a team and encourage one another toward excellence.

Make sure to check out opportunities to create a retrospective workshop. You can find plenty of exercises online at several websites, including www.tastycup cakes.org, www.gogamestorm.com, and www.innova tiongames.com.

## Agile Team Questions

1. What happened during the last iteration?
2. What went well, and what can we celebrate as a success?
3. What are things that didn't go so well, and how can we improve the next sprint?

# Chapter 16

## Wash, Rinse,

## Repeat, Win!

The sounds of celebration are wafting through the jungle. The melodic beats of the drums rise and fall as if the jungle is alive with one heart and one breath. The leaders in the business are popping their heads out of their windows and doors, all in the direction of your Agile Team. Something is brewing in the jungle, and an atmosphere of healthy anxiety is permeating the landscape like a thin fog. Early reports say that the Agile Team now has all the elements necessary for a successful rollout of Scrum, and some of the Tribes in the business are getting excited about the possibility of productivity increases and better communication and collaboration, as well as a unification of production throughout the different Tribes in the jungle. The gears of change are meshing, and it all began with you.

Agile management can be as simple or complex as you desire. Some things to think about include the following:

- Define as a Team which particulars of an Agile framework will be implemented into your culture.
- Define rules, processes, procedures, guidelines, and standards for your teams (i.e., standard meeting guidelines, estimation standards, communication channels).
- Define project members' roles and responsibilities (i.e., who is responsible for what). (See Figure 16.1.)
- Define goals and plans for measuring the success of a project (i.e., what makes a product rollout successful).
- Define and promote iteration standards that are necessary for your company's delivery cycle (i.e., discovery, backlog grooming, Daily Scrum).

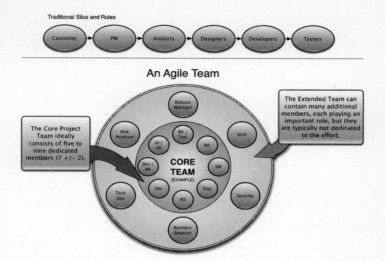

**Figure 16.1  An Agile Team Diagrammed by Roles and Responsibilities**

- Define a communication strategy of releases to all necessary business units.
- Define and understand your company's culture (see Chapter 17).

In the continual effort for you to implement Agile processes in your organization, you will need to be cognizant of being absolutely consistent with your

*Wash, Rinse, Repeat, Win!*

communication to all the different business units. Agile and Scrum in itself do not tell us how to do software and product development or prescribe processes for business analysis or product management. Agile is not a project management tool. It is simply a framework that can fit around the specific nuances of your organization. With that in mind, a healthy balance of transparency and disclosure will garner trust and willingness from the other business leaders as you grow your influence and success with Agile within the already established processes that your business has. Your best weapon is continuing to read and learn. Your best defense against being ineffective in Agile is a direct result of how much you continually educate yourself and arm yourself with the knowledge that comes from others who are far more wise and successful than yourself. Remember, this book isn't prescriptive, and it does not have all the answers! Your experience, skill, and common sense will augment many of the suggestions I've made. My hope is that this will be a great starting point for increasing agility, value, and fun at your company or team!

## Leader Questions

1. Am I willing to set the bar high and set goals for my team and my company?
2. Am I willing to be a patient Servant Leader who will do what it takes to be successful?
3. Am I willing to be empathetic and show humility as a fellow learner?

*Wash, Rinse, Repeat, Win!*

# Chapter 17

# Team and Business

# Cultural Dynamics—

# Team Science™

Business leaders, executives, and managers must understand that team and business culture affect productivity, sustainability, and employee satisfaction. We are no longer in the manufacturing age where each employee is simply a cog in a big wheel. As a Leader, you hired people for their problem-solving abilities, technical aptitude, and fit; not for their good looks (I hope).

You want to ensure that each team has been enabled, equipped, and designed optimally. You want to ensure that each team member communicates, collaborates, and works well with others. Finally, you want to make sure that all impediments to productivity and cultural dysfunctions are removed.

How is it possible to do all this and create high-performing teams? The best way that I've found is through a cultural and team assessment. As a business transformation coach and manager, I want to know where there are gaps within team collaboration and communication. I want to understand how to engage intentionally with each team member and how to optimize each team member's potential, or strengths. When I say that I want companies to hire the right candidates and have the right levers to pull when building new or augmenting existing teams, I am not talking about resumes and recommendations. I want to definitively know whether candidates are exactly the right cultural fit for my company and team.

I've used several assessments in the past that have fallen flat on their faces. The most effective team- and cultural-assessment tool built specifically for use within the team context is Team Science™ (www.myai.org). This tool has allowed me to be far more successful as

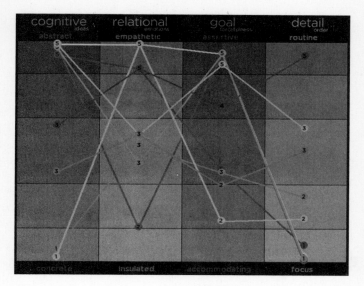

**Figure 17.1   A Team's Cultural Plot and Dynamics using the Team Science™ Platform**

a coach and consultant to my clients in that it quickly allows me to assess the cultural dynamics, deficiencies, and opportunities in each team I work with.

Team Science™ (Figure 17.1) helps businesses and teams by:

- Optimizing each employee and revealing or her potential and strengths.

**97**

- Enabling managers and executives to build the right teams for the right projects.
- Allowing hiring managers to recruit and employ the right candidates based on cultural and strategic fit.
- Increasing awareness of team dynamics and collaboration styles.
- Helping with decision making and conflict resolution.
- Focusing on how to choose the right Leaders.
- Encouraging you to empower your employees.

## Example Case

I have utilized the Team Science™ solution with many of my clients. One of my most memorable occasions was helping a medium-sized company fundamentally change their organization. After having the entire organization take the assessment, we quickly understood why there were not only problems in their delivery of products on time, but also the apparent gaps that created miscommunication between teams.

We did five things with this company in the span of 1.5 months:

1. We optimized each team and moved employees around to functional roles they were best suited for (i.e., moving a business analyst with a knack for detail into a quality-engineer role).
2. We assigned employees new responsibilities we knew they would thrive and be successful at.
3. We hired three new employees based on cultural fit to the company and not on their resume alone.
4. We increased productivity in every single team by allowing each team member to fully understand how to best engage with their fellow team members.
5. We improved almost all employees' work–life balance and job satisfaction (survey of job satisfaction sent out two months after employment of Team Science™).

Team Science™ has been the best instrument in my tool belt as a coach and consultant. It has allowed me to engage correctly with my clients, optimize their human capital, and empower and enable the right leaders to lead their company to high-performance. A major win!

# Chapter 18

## Scrum of Scrums

I love daily stand-ups. I love quick and efficient meetings that enable everyone to get on the same page and understand the work that lies ahead for the day. I love being able to communicate the team's daily goal and the highest-priority items that need to receive immediate attention. Most of this happens in the Daily Scrum, but there is some information that needs to be disseminated to managers or other teams. If you have multiple teams, cross-team issues, or other dependencies that need to be discussed, then it may be a cue to have a so-called Scrum of Scrums.

A Scrum of Scrums is a Scrum team made up of representatives from each of several other teams. In multiple code base teams, this is absolutely essential. I've consulted with IT departments that have multiple teams utilizing different code bases and have different managers for each team. How is it possible to keep up with all of the information shared between those teams, and the goals each team works toward, with their interdependencies and complex interplay of resources? Again, you need a Scrum of Scrums.

A Scrum of Scrums meeting can happen right after a regular Scrum meeting. Like any regular Scrum team, the Scrum of Scrums works iteratively to deliver value in the form of removing organizational and cross-functional team obstacles, dependencies, and conflicts. Just like a regular Scrum stand-up, the purpose of the Scrum of Scrums meeting is to resolve escalated obstacles or resolve dependencies between teams, as well as to document and follow up on any necessary communication between managers and developer leads on each of the respective teams.

## Example Case

I found this quick stand-up to be of great value in my experience with one client. It enabled me to communicate to all the lead developers and managers the overall goals and enterprise-wide needs, as well as to document and note issues the teams needed to resolve. This daily check-in often provides valuable information to me because, remember, my primary job as an Agile coach is to remove obstacles to success! The interplay between cross-functional teams at times can be as complex as it is cumbersome. A meeting of the minds once each day can open up the flow of communication needed to break down the barriers that inhibit absolute productivity.

**103**

*Scrum of Scrums*

# Chapter 19

## Thirty-Second

### Scrum Elevator Pitch

I can be verbose at times. The way that I explain things can be intricately detailed and sometimes too technical for my audience. I'm still learning how to compose and communicate things at a consumable level for my target audience, which made this book a great exercise in conciseness!

I am often asked what Agile or Scrum is all about. It is crucial that my target audience be assured that I do know what I'm talking about and that I can effectively communicate with them. I find that the following exercise is also of value for anyone who wants to accurately represent his or her company. Ideally, your company has clearly defined its mission and values to you so that you can easily tell others about the organization and why you work for it. I would hope that you enjoy the place where you work and that you'd be more than willing to speak about your company in a way that tells your audience its mission, vision, goals, and values that you not only adhere to but also enjoy following. If your company hasn't successfully instilled its value proposition upon you, then that is another chapter for another day.

So, suppose you find yourself in a position in which the president of your company asks you, "Tell me what this Agile/Scrum thing is all about." You have thirty seconds. Go!

You start off explaining that Scrum is a framework that allows the company to deliver highest-priority software quickly and efficiently. This process is iterative in nature, and there is frequent inspection and adaptation of the product as it is built. The management and leadership of the process encourage teamwork, accountability, and servant leadership.

You go on to say that the Scrum framework allows your teams to continue to adapt to the changing market conditions, enables customer feedback and insight, and brings in the best talent desiring to work in a successful environment building great products. Not only is your president impressed, but he or she will most likely want to speak more with you about implementing Agile best practices company-wide.

## Example Case

In the beginning of my journey in software development in the mid-1990s, I had the unique opportunity to shadow an experienced supporter of new-age software development (the beginnings of what is now Agile). I was consuming and reading as much as I could about different practices in software development, and I was learning a ton about different ways to divert from the typical waterfall practices. It was so incredible for me to see the effects of what he was implementing, and it seemed like a lot of positive increases in productivity were happening. As a project manager at the time, I was drinking the Agile Kool-Aid by the gallon.

One day, I was approached by my CTO, who asked me what I knew about the framework and theory around our new software development practices. I froze, and I failed—epically. I simply didn't do justice to the new processes and practices that we were employing. I knew essentially what we were doing but couldn't explain it in a clear and concise manner. Thankfully, he understood even though I was thoroughly embarrassed. That episode taught me that not only did I need to know more about what I was doing, but I also, through experience, needed to be able to give practical reasons for the ways we were doing things. The point is, understand your work. Continue to learn, and continue to grow in your Agile journey!

## Chapter 20

# Understanding

# Requirements

One of the many struggles that proponents of Agile face is the changing-requirements churn. The story is the same: funds are allocated to the tune of $3 million, product specs are built out, requirements are built, a timeline is proposed, work begins—and then the Product Owner or stakeholders say they need to change things in the requirements, or the market has changed. You are now in month 9 of a 15-month project. Wow, how did that happen? Fortunately, for many of us, Agile is exactly the approach that manages change very well because it includes a flexible change-management process.

**109**

Requirements change for various reasons, as we all know: a stakeholder realizes that she missed a requirement or the requirements are missing a feature, issues and bugs are identified, market demands change, Product Owners don't realize what they actually needed, or just plain old politics create problems. The two greatest points I want to make are that we do not want to prevent change from happening (requirements change!), and we must allow the business or stakeholders to prioritize the changes. To allow the business to change requirements is something that we can adjust for easily. Freezing requirements early in the life cycle prohibits the business from getting what it wants and also guarantees that the development team does not make what the stakeholders want.

An individual Product Owner needs to be the single point of authority and must understand that he or she is where the buck stops. Often, there are multiple Product Owners from various business units. Regardless, they need to sign off on the prioritization of the requirements that go into the backlog. The development team, in turn, needs to be responsible for taking the time to estimate the effort and giving the business a healthy time line for the changes that will go into each sprint. What the business and stakeholders will appreciate and find value in is your commitment to the business, allowing them to make the changes necessary to build the best product. You can add icing to the requirements-changing cake in that you'll hold Scrum meetings to give the business reports on productivity, issues and blockers, and needs from development.

The way you communicate your commitment to the business will not only build rapport and trust within your organization but also allow the flexibility and adaptability of Agile that makes the methodology so successful. Stakeholders get the constant feedback that they need to make their executive decisions, and they have control over the scope in that they can change requirements and priorities, add new requirements, and modify the backlog. They also have control over the changed schedule, funding the changes through budget constraints, and making sure they get the changes they need—according to the number of iterations you've told them it will take to make the changes.

I hope you can see where this is going. The process can be heavy and time intensive, but it need not always

be that way. The core element is allowing the communication channels to be open and change to be made if
the business needs it. Your job is to make sure stakeholders are reminded that they must be responsible for
both making decisions and providing information and
requirements in a timely manner. They must also be
responsible for the prioritization of the requirements.
On the other hand, your commitment to the business is
to communicate your time constraints and requirements
questions in a timely manner and give the business as
much feedback as necessary to allow the players to
make product decisions and trade-offs.

## Example Case

One of my recent clients had one development team
serving five different business units. The workload was
intense! The various departments were always changing
requirements due to market fluctuations and the customer feedback they garnered from a month-to-month
basis. They had no single Product Owner and many
varying opinions about how each product should be
built. What was the solution I recommended? Creating
what I call a product alignment team. (See Figure 20.1.)

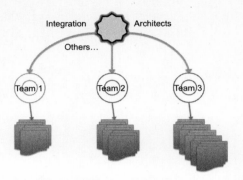

**Figure 20.1 The Product Alignment Team Coordinates Work between Multiple Teams**

This team was made up of all the various different Product Owners from their respective departments. They met weekly to discuss the priority of what was going into the enterprise backlog of work for the single Agile team to tackle. During these meetings, they could change requirements, add or subtract features, and mess around all they wanted. The final deliverable entity from those weekly meetings was simple: a bullet list of prioritized changes and work that needed to be done by the team. What was an unruly feedback loop from five different Product Owners became a single feed filter of distilled features in order of business value.

*Understanding Requirements*

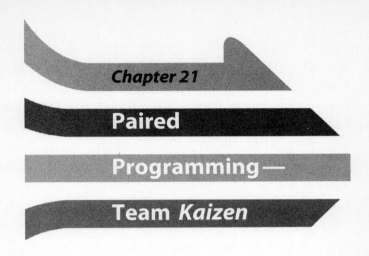

# Chapter 21

## Paired

## Programming—

## Team *Kaizen*

I've received numerous questions about the engineering principle of paired programming, often centered on its feasibility and "real" benefits. For many people, this inquiry is simply a probing question and not something that they'll ever act on or employ. Budget constraints cause businesses to balk at such misunderstood waste: "I mean, seriously, why have two programmers work on a workstation when two independent programmers can do twice as much?" I get it; it's a tough question to answer and an even harder practice to test in your organization. Imagine speaking with the president of your IT department and telling her that you are going to slow down production a little bit to have two developers work on the same piece of work. How long do you think you'll be working for that company? But ideally, management will be very informed and open to your suggestion—you'll keep your job and be recognized for coming up with a great idea.

I was recently given an article written by Stuart Wray[1] that really helped my explanation of paired programming, and I have leveraged his writing in this chapter. In terms of my own experience, I've not only seen it work but have deployed this engineering practice with great success. There are pros and cons to paired programming. The most obvious negative is the thought that "one guy programs and the other just sits there." Well, we can only hope that is not happening in your environment, but let me offer six reasons why paired programming works:

[1]Stuart Wray, "How Pair Programming Really Works." www.computer.org/cms/Computer.org/ComputingNow/homepage/mostread/MostRead-SW-PairProgrammingReallyWorks.pdf.

*The Agile Pocket Guide*

1. Paired programmers can ask the right questions of each other to draw out crucial knowledge and bring about moments of epiphany (i.e., the "aha!" moment).

2. Paired programmers can catch problems early (e.g., if the code is syntactically correct but semantically wrong, or where there is a fault in the design itself).

3. Paired programmers give a fresh perspective to old code when re-paired with other developers in consistent and frequent intervals. Research has found that the same pair of programmers working together over time tends to notice (and fails to notice) similar things (a condition called *pair fatigue*).

4. Paired programmers give each other *pair pressure*, the feeling of wanting to do the best and staying away from poor practices.

5. Paired programmers can give better estimates of level of effort (LOE) over time as they realize their own level of expertise within the group of developers. This also helps when you have a particular developer who is well experienced

*Paired Programming—Team Kaizen*

with specific areas of need and can fix or address them quickly.

**6.** Paired programmers create team cohesiveness and greater knowledge sharing (team *kaizen*, or continuous learning cycles).

## Example Case

To me, the most important point about paired programming is the last point in the list above: team *kaizen*. In one of my experiences with a client, an environment had been created that really appreciated cross-functional teams and utilized knowledge sharing for the benefit of the whole team. Consider this: if only one developer knows how to deploy code to production and that person leaves the business unexpectedly, how will you survive? The paired-programming aspect of business allows the entire team to have the shared experience of building and coding all aspects of your product. This not only allows them to know more about your product and business, but also helps them to improve each other along the way. It took a bit of time for the business to see the real value of paying for two developers to do one piece of work, but the metrics after 12 sprints astounded everyone! We had improved time to market by 20 percent. We had decreased quality assurance time by almost 50 percent! The biggest win for us was that we had no critical point of failure in resources. Our team members were learning each other's job functions, and almost every team member knew how to deploy code to production!

## Chapter 22

# Measuring

## a Working Product

One of the things a team needs to clarify for itself is what it means to be *done*. As team members continue along the Agile path, they are supposed to demo the product and then retrospect the sprint. The demo process signifies that the stakeholders have working software, product, or something they can use. But, let's be real here: there are times when you have a sprint that won't include a demo-able piece of software or product (though we talked about how this can be avoided in Chapter 14). Regardless, how do we measure that the software is working? Do we define it through

**121**

the fact that our critical test paths work and the code is running? Maybe we should look into how we define *working*, or *done*.

One thing to take into consideration is how different teams define *done*. A developer will not have the same definition as a QA analyst, a database developer, or a systems or business analyst. To begin, sometimes it's easier to figure out what something is by first looking and defining what it is not.

One of the worst ways to measure whether something can be classified as *working software* is by meeting documented specifications. This may sound contrary to popular belief, but often the specifications have fatal flaws in them and the product may not exactly do what is necessary for greatest value to the business. Revenue is another way by which many companies measure whether the software is working; however, as I've found in the past, market fluctuations affect revenue so often that it is hard to create a real baseline. Sometimes companies use surveys to find out whether their users are happy with the software, but users often change their minds about the same piece of software depending on their needs and even emotions at the time.

Given this information, how should the term *working software* be defined? The bottom line is that the software should meet the identified business or mission capabilities needed and defined by the business (i.e., product features that the business prioritizes as highest value). (See Figure 22.1.) The identification of the technical and operational requirements needs to be identified next, along with a plan built to schedule the delivery of the product through iterations. The *done* aspect of this is that at the end of each sprint, the customer can see how the features built can be tied

**Figure 22.1   Value Should Be Derived from Every Part of the Agile Process**

*Measuring a Working Product*

directly to the mission-critical features of the product or strategy.

To say that a product is working is not a helpful statement to make. Far too often I've heard this statement: "It's working and the feature launch was successful—well, we built it and the code works, doesn't it?" And then, in fact, we've had to spend time repeatedly changing the product to meet the business needs. Having a definition of *working product* enables all parties involved to know the measurement for success. Having this type of definition up front will allow everyone to see whether the product is meeting the real value from the business.

## Example Case

Early on in my career I couldn't have told you how to truly measure *done*. I could give you horror stories recounting conversations with clients or business folks around the so-called finished product. "Hey, that doesn't really do what we wanted!" "What made you guys think that this feature is complete?" Ah, those memories are long gone. But what I did learn early on is exactly the point that I hope you didn't miss in Chapter 12: the Product Owner and the Agile Team must own and understand the definition of *done* for each sprint. This definition must be understood throughout the team and can even be included in the theme or goal for the sprint. Depending on what type of project your team is working on, the definition of *done* can be a screenshot of final design or even a defined piece of functionality written on the wall. Regardless, the definition of *done* needs to be apparent and visible for all to see.

*Measuring a Working Product*

# Chapter 23

# Technical Debt

## Is a Progress Killer!

When I work with clients, there comes a time when we look under the hood at the current product they have been building. We always find there has been a ton of code that has been passed over, saved for later, or just commented out. This does not include all the extra pieces of code that just sit around all over the place! One of the many issues that a development team must start to think about is how technical debt adds up.

Technical debt is anything that should have been done as part of a development process but wasn't. This includes test cases, bugs that were not resolved, unrefactored code, missing documentation, and even process debt (gaps). This debt is like any other debt—you keep paying on it. By incurring this debt, the team and systems are mortgaging your future in the following ways:

- Technical debt slows down our velocity.
- Technical debt causes more issues in the long run due to "work-arounds."
- Technical debt breaks processes and creates instability in releases.
- Technical debt causes uncertainty.

Educating team members and others in business about technical debt is the first step in overcoming it. In order to create a quality product, the team must find a sustainable pace that does not incur debt. Quite possibly, you'll have to slow down the pace of the team a bit to ensure there's enough leeway (in time) to fix the technical debt in each sprint. The business translates this to mean: "It looks like we won't get as many features as we want." That is okay. The education for everyone on the team and the business is the fact that it is exponentially more expensive to fix bugs after a product launch.

## Example Case

For a recent client we had established a healthy cadence and product release schedule. In project A, we were deploying code to production every two weeks and the business was happy. Project B was in the works as well. It was falling behind, incurring terrible technical debt, and it seemed that every sprint was geared to just fixing the code from the previous iteration.

I sat down with the Product Owner and let her know that we needed to take a serious look at what was happening. We needed to slow our production down a bit so we could better understand what was happening. Taking a feature or two off the table for the next four iterations (eight weeks) we succeeded in several things:

- We finished all bug remediation before completing a sprint.

*Technical Debt Is a Progress Killer!*

- We found the problems in the process that allowed technical debt to get into the system in the first place.
- We attacked technical debt as part of our *done* definition, and a story wasn't completely done unless it had been refactored.

## Chapter 24

# Oh Kanban!

Well-informed practitioners of Agile sometimes talk with me about the Kanban method and ask me whether Kanban is better than Scrum and which one I use (the Japanese word *kanban* means *signboard* or *signal card*). Interestingly enough, I've been going to more and more conferences that have leaders who speak about Kanban. I write a lot about Scrum because it's what I've been using and have found successful with my clients. I am, however, a very big proponent of Kanban if a mature organization can use it wisely and effectively, and if the business and technology units can work cohesively. Sound too ideological for you? Maybe, but for Kanban to be successful, the wheels of an organization must be well-greased and communication channels must be wide open and transparent.

The main difference between Kanban and Scrum is that Scrum development moves to the rhythm of Timeboxed increments, usually two to four weeks, and are bookended by meetings and a sprint review. Kanban, on the other hand, does not have Timeboxed increments or any task estimates. Scrum tracks velocity, while Kanban tracks the flow of items moving through the work in process (WIP) and the total cycle time for an item to move through the development cycle to deployment. (See Figure 24.1.) In Scrum, a master owns the process; in Kanban, the team owns the process. The people who

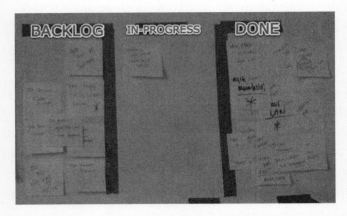

**Figure 24.1   My Personal Kanban Board at Home**

*The Agile Pocket Guide*

are proponents of Scrum are looking for a consistent cadence in the sprints, and those using Kanban look at the flow of minimal marketable features. In a sense, the flow of work in Kanban is that the team simply takes the next task and works on it through the process. If there is a particularly limiting factor in Kanban, it is simply the amount of WIP a team can handle at any given time (e.g., four tasks total at any time).

My experience has been that Kanban is a great way to manage workloads for teams. (See Figure 24.2.) The Kanban construct allows teams to pick up work as long as it doesn't cause problems downstream. For example, one can easily find a bottleneck in the process if QA cannot keep up with the amount of WIP that the developers are working on. While Kanban can be incredibly efficient, the organization must have a deep commitment to continual improvement (*kaizen*).

The biggest caveat is that Kanban must not be used by itself. A system like Kanban has to accompany other best practices to augment the agility that Kanban affords. Since Kanban is very agile and efficient in its responsiveness to the changes in customer needs, other processes must be in place to give framework to some

*Oh Kanban!*

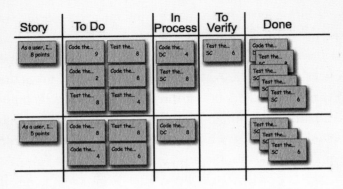

| Story | To Do | | In Process | To Verify | Done |
|---|---|---|---|---|---|
| As a user, I...<br>8 points | Code the...<br>9 | Test the...<br>8 | Code the...<br>DC 4 | Test the...<br>SC 6 | Code the...<br>D<br>Test the...<br>SC<br>Test the...<br>SC<br>Test the...<br>SC<br>Test the...<br>SC 6 |
| | Code the...<br>2 | Code the...<br>8 | Test the...<br>SC 8 | | |
| | Test the...<br>8 | Test the...<br>4 | | | |
| As a user, I...<br>5 points | Code the...<br>8 | Test the...<br>8 | Code the...<br>DC 8 | | Test the...<br>SC<br>Test the...<br>SC<br>Test the...<br>SC 6 |
| | Code the...<br>4 | Code the...<br>6 | | | |

**Figure 24.2 An Advanced Kanban Board Example from Mike Cohn** *Source*: **Mike Cohn,** *Task Boards.* **www.mountaingoatsoftware.com/scrum/task-boards.**

organizational needs that Kanban cannot provide solutions for. I highly recommend finding other resources around Kanban that will give your team the structure it needs to build great software in a Kanban environment.

## Example Case

When I think about Kanban, one client immediately comes to mind. I had about a two-month engagement with this company, and it wanted to transform its current nonprocess into an Agile software development shop.

Sounds heavy, right? Well, not as much as you may think. Since this development shop was small, it was a lot more flexible and adaptable to change than a large Fortune 500 company would be. The company had to make changes quickly to its websites as market fluctuations occurred. After a couple of presentations and discovery sessions with the development team, we decided on a solution that didn't lock team members into any specific development length, or sprints. What they needed was the ability to focus on features of work that could, if needed, be changed by the Product Owner in midflight. The Kanban structure worked well because at any given moment a course correction made by the Product Owner could be accepted and worked on within minutes. What was also great was that we created a simple Kanban board, and were able to visibly see flow of work as it progressed through the lanes. Easy! In terms of our flow, it was as simple as replacing one piece of work with another, as long as the total number of features didn't go over our WIP limit. This company found value in the fact that it could track items being done and feels that all the team members were fully utilized. A win-win situation!

**135**

*Oh Kanban!*

# Chapter 25

## Personal *Kaizen*—
## More on Servant
## Leadership

I believe it is vastly important to ground oneself in the power and position of being a Servant Leader for your company and team. It really is the most rewarding place to put oneself. It many ways, it might seem counterintuitive to the idea that only the hard-working, tough-as-nails, demanding, authority figures get promoted. In my experience, it is exactly the opposite. As I have seen time and time again, the ones who place their team, their fellow employees, and others before themselves are the ones who reap more rewarding personal and professional gain. They don't do it for personal gain, but rather, the personal gain is a perk that comes with serving others.

I believe that personal character isn't taught, but rather it is grown over time. The more time you spend on personal *kaizen*, or self-improvement to help others, the more fulfilling and rewarding your work and life will be. The following is what I consider to be the Top 10 Personal Skills for a Servant Leader. I suggest you read each one and let it resonate within you.

1. **Communicative and social**—A Servant Leader must be able to communicate well with all people, teams, and business levels. Understanding your communication style is imperative to knowing how to engage effectively with people from all walks of life and backgrounds!

2. **Facilitative**—A Servant Leader must be able to lead, manage, and even coach teams of people to work collaboratively, cohesively, and effectively. A great facilitator knows how to grease the wheels of productivity in a stagnant group.

You also know how to make meetings less boring and more energizing by utilizing an array of facilitation techniques to keep everyone moving forward.

3. **Assertive**—A Servant Leader must be able to ensure the right things on which to focus and the right concepts and principles to follow. You must be a voice of reason and authority when needed. You must be able to make the tough calls and be a respected supporter and voice of those who may not have the gumption to speak up.

4. **Situationally aware**—A Servant Leader must be the first to notice issues as they arise and be tactful enough to address them when needed. You must know when to take a coaching role, or when to delegate issues to upper management. A Servant Leader who monitors the pulse of a situation can often preempt conflicts or issues before they reach a boiling point.

5. **Enthusiastic**—A Servant Leader must be high energy, with focus. While many great leaders have approached their role through their ethos

**139**

of passivity, they share common ground with their limitless energy toward the goals they have set for themselves and their people. People want to follow an enthusiastic leader. People will rally around your enthusiasm.

6. **Continually improving**—A Servant Leader must be one who lives a life of continuous improvement, and helps drive continuous improvement in his or her team, business, and personal life. You didn't stop learning after you got your high school or college degree, did you? Tons of learning opportunities occur every day in the office. Make them count.

7. **Conflict resolution**—A Servant Leader must be able to handle conflict well and be able to facilitate discussion, alternatives, or different approaches when conflict arises. A clear head, with your emotions in check, is an obvious prerequisite for this. Conflict resolution isn't easy. Certainly, being situationally aware and preempting conflict would be a plus here.

8. **Attitude of empowerment**—A Servant Leader is one who coaches individuals and teams toward

self-organization. This means that you must allow individuals to have the right balance of autonomy, self-transcendence, and management oversight. You aren't in the manufacturing days anymore. People aren't just cogs in a big wheel. They need to feel like they can self-manage at certain levels and have the ability to figure out how they will do the work, and work within the frameworks of managers who set the goals of what needs to get done. You should be the enabler who removes any impediments to individual and team success.

9. **Attitude of transparency**—A Servant Leader must desire to foster to a healthy dose of disclosure and transparency about practices and processes in the business. Transparency also grows trust between your team and the rest of the organization. This isn't a call to build a lot of status reports. Rather, it is call to monitor the amount of value-added information that needs to be open and available for the business to base decisions on. A great way to begin is to have candid conversations with management

*Personal **Kaizen**—More on Servant Leadership*

to know exactly what they need to know, focus on that, and then iterate and improve as you go.

**10.** **Coach mentality**—Remember a great coach of your little league team? Or a great mentor during your younger school days? Those people not only led by example, but they also added pressure as necessary to help you improve. Coaches put emotional capital into the game. They go above and beyond the call of duty. What is it that you need to do to encourage, mentor, and lead your team?

All of these suggestions are simply just that. In reality, this list is a big challenge for many. To begin, take each idea presented here and focus on it for a week. Write down the pragmatic steps that you need to take to start being a better Servant Leader. Begin slowly, and then inspect, adapt, and improve over time.

## Chapter 26

# Team *Kaizen*—

## Practicing Agile

Agile is all about inspecting, adapting, and improving upon findings to better yourself, your team, and your business. I would say that Agile isn't so much the *doing*, but rather the *being*. In other words, for me, Agile is a lifestyle choice to continually move toward greatness through iterative and incremental steps.

Many organizations "do Agile." They have the right disciplines, the right ceremonies, and even the right artifacts. They then put a stamp on it and call it "Agile." Often, when they get to this point they proclaim that they've reached the pinnacle of success and get set in their ways. That doesn't seem very Agile at all, does it?

We call a lot of things *practices*, and what we really mean by that word is *things we do*. Just because we're doing them doesn't mean we're improving along the way. Let's take it a step further. Often you hear the adage, "practice makes perfect." I disagree.

In my experience, the saying "practice makes permanent" is more like it. Just because you're practicing something doesn't mean you're practicing the right thing. Let's say you're working on your golf swing. You could practice that particular movement over and over again and what you'll have is poor form permanently etched into your muscle memory. See my point?

Having thoughtful deliberation about what your team and company are practicing is at the essence of Agile. Instead of just "doing" or "practicing," thoughtfully deliberate about what you're practicing. Don't forget to take opportunities to learn and relearn. Here is a list of things to start doing to improve your team and company:

- **Start small and continue to execute**—Take the basic fundamentals of iterative development and practice it with your team. As improvement and change begin to take hold, try something new. Always remember to assess changes in retrospect. Are they working well? If so, continue on. If not, find out why, or discontinue!

- **Review and understand other processes and methodologies, and employ as needed**—There are always opportunities to leverage other techniques to provide value to the current way in which you are doing things. Google "Learn more Agile software development methods" and see what's out there for you to use.

- **Experience the outside world**—Go to conferences, meet-ups, and local gatherings of professionals. To grow your professional skills and keep increasing your value to your team and company, you have to learn and relearn technologies and methodologies. Put in a little time and money and you could find yourself across the table from someone far more influential and smarter than you are. Take those opportunities to network and grow!

- **Read, read, read**—Read blogs to stay up to date with industry leaders. What are they saying? Read books by powerful authors in various industries.

*Team Kaizen—Practicing Agile*

Don't like paperbacks? Download them to your electronic reader!

- **Start a company interest group**—You'd be surprised at how many people are interested in making work a better place. Find your niche. Start a book club. Kick-start the company by grabbing influential people to help make your company or team just a little bit better.

- **Start writing, blogging, and tweeting**—Start writing down your personal experiences in your profession. There is a lot you can learn through expounding on your experiences. You'll also meet like-minded people who are on the same journey as you are. Follow experienced professionals on Twitter. See what they are reading. Leverage their vast knowledge to change your reality at work and at home.

*The Agile Pocket Guide*

# Chapter 27

## Product *Kaizen*—

## The Value Driver

## for Your Product

We've talked in Chapter 7 about how important Product Owners are in the whole Agile process. This is still true. This will always be true! Whether you call this individual a *Product Owner* or something entirely different doesn't remove the tremendous importance of this role for a company or team. I like to call this individual the *Value Driver* to the team. The Value Driver is the person responsible for determining what the team is going to build.

Simply put, the Value Driver should be able to quickly answer the following questions:

- Why are we building this and what problem do we intend it to solve?
- Who is the primary user of our product?
- What is important for the primary user?
- What are the issues or constraints we should be aware of?

I've often been asked about what I believe a Value Driver should be like in terms of character and skill set. I've even taken an entire year and have primarily spoken about the Value Driver at several conferences and meet ups. Here are my Top 10 Value Driver Qualities and Characteristics:

1. **Engaged leadership**—The best Value Drivers are engaged in the entire process. Disengaged leaders find themselves outside of the process quickly. Engaged Value Drivers are natural leaders who lead their team through decisions and make it apparent to their teams that they are committed to not only the process, but the final product as well.

2. **Available within reason**—The best Value Drivers are available to the team, but within reason. There is something about collocating oneself within the team so team members have zero walls to climb in order to receive feedback and potentially daily guidance. The availability can come at a cost, however, with an immature team whose members lack the accountability and responsibility of building the needed project. Be tactful here and give a healthy balance between availability and baby-sitting. Sometimes helping team members help themselves can create a partnership between the team and the Value Driver that speaks, loud and clear, of productivity!

3. **Informed about the product**—The best Value Drivers know the product inside and out. Newly minted employees need not apply here. Subject matter experts on not only the product but also the market will find themselves the best prepared for giving updated feedback and guidance to a team. Understanding beyond the product can help here as well, but at the core of

**149**

the Value Driver role is the ability to intimately know and understand the product a team needs to build.

4. **Empowered through humility**—The best Value Drivers are the end-all. They have been given the official right to make executive calls on product direction and feature-set. They have been granted this permission and power through their ability to lead with humility. They don't take their power for granted, because they know that as quickly as it was granted, it can be taken away. They show their humility through history, continually making the right choices and correcting poor product choices through due diligence and research. They intimately know their power comes at a price, because in the end, their decision-making power can cause a company to grow or to fall into obscurity with poor product development.

5. **Prepared and responsible**—The best Value Drivers are always prepared. Like good scouts, they come to the ceremonial meetings prepared and ready to make decisions and take action.

Preparation is key here because it is easily apparent when people are not prepared. Value Drivers gain trust from the development team because the team knows that they are always prepared and responsible for the outcome of the product specifications and features. Development teams can be fickle, and often they will go to the nearest "prepared" individuals for better guidance and direction if "official" Value Drivers aren't responsible to their role.

6. **Knowledgeable about history**—The best Value Drivers are crafted through time. They have been around, seen the ups and downs of the product life cycles, and understand how the customer base values the product. These guys and gals are old guard, but not old in the sense of not being up to date on the market and products. They are old guard in the sense that they have a firm foundation of knowledge to pull from when decisions need to be made. They know the historical path of poor product development and poor product launches. They've been there.

**151**

*Product Kaizen—The Value Driver for Your Product*

And sometimes, they were the reason. But they learned and use that experience to create even better products and services.

7. **Communicative in nature**—The best Value Drivers are natural communicators. They know how to leverage communication to get their point across so they can give undiluted guidance and direction to a development team. They know how to reach not only the customer base, but know how to speak the development language. Developers respect, trust, and look forward to working with communicative Value Drivers. They respect Value Drivers because Value Drivers know how to speak on the level of the developer and may themselves even know how to code and develop!

8. **Collaborative by choice**—The best Value Drivers are team players. They value team members as the gears through which the product moves as it is built, and they collaborate effectively with the team, providing timely and valuable feedback, during that process. Collaboration is a choice, and many Value Drivers aren't good

collaborators. It takes time, it takes effort, and it takes commitment. Do you have it?

9. **Agile in all things**—The best Value Drivers are flexible, in all things. They understand that software development is not a hardened process but fluid, all the time. They work collaboratively with the team when changes must be made. They don't get angry when previously unknown impediments and constraints come up. They are flexible because they have done the work ahead of time: a prioritized backlog, daily communication with the teams, intense research on the product and market. They are only agile because they are prepared.

10. **Fun and reasonable**—The best Value Drivers are fun. Period. Serious people need not apply. There are times when teams are against the wall. We get it! But ultimately, nobody wants to be led by a humorless individual. Be fun. Bring life back into product development. Your team, your boss, and even your company will thank you for it.

*Product Kaizen—The Value Driver for Your Product*

# Chapter 28

## Cultural *Kaizen*—

## Leadership in

## Dynamic Team

## Cultures

Here's the hard truth: *You are not as effective as you possibly could be.*

Let's be even more honest for a moment, shall we? As an organizational consultant and Agile coach, I know first-hand what it's like going into a company and not having the faintest clue as to what they are *really* like.

Yes, I got the "brief," I've had the meetings, I even had a few one-on-one's, but I really haven't gotten the whole story.

And neither have you, I would venture. You and I both know that it's really difficult to get a solid pulse on the cultural and team dynamics at play—sometimes we're simply flying blind.

Being a Leader is all about helping businesses and teams thrive. The top impediments to doing this are often:

- Executive management buy-in.
- Dependencies and constraints on complex systems and designs.
- Business culture.

The management buy-in often stems from mistrust of the process, the value, and the how. More specifically, how is Agile is going to work in *my* business, *my* culture, *my* environment? Complex systems? We can move through a slow process of integration, modularization, and candid conversations with different business units and break this down into something that logically flows. The culture? Now that's the hard one.

The struggles of cultural change are typically found in these challenges:

- It is absolutely hard to incite positive change into a culture.
- Teams and management cannot agree on the right approach to change culture.
- Management is leery of widespread changes to processes.
- Team dysfunctions are obvious, but the core reasons these dysfunctions appear are hard to pin down.
- And so on and so on . . .

If you want to change culture and lead teams to success, you need the best instruments in your tool belt. You will be far better equipped if you understand how to coach team members through change. Knowing how to engage with your team will be the best starting point to being more effective. You need to start at the people level and have the right tools to help you clarify the culture so that you can truly create positive and lasting change.

It's time to build an Agile Culture, not just an agile method for your team. In order to understand your influence and leadership with your team, refer to my 10-point leadership checklist:

1. How and where do I have influence?
2. Where can I improve my people skills?
3. Do I have a positive outlook?
4. Do I see evidence of personal growth and self-discipline?
5. Do I inspire others toward personal *kaizen*?
6. How are my problem-solving skills?
7. Do I refuse to accept the status quo?
8. Do I have a big-picture mindset?
9. Do I know how to best engage with my team?
10. Am I leveraging the true potential in my team members?

I am absolutely passionate about creating Agile Cultures within businesses. I talk about this in Chapter 17 when I discuss the use of Team Science™ to better understand the cultural dynamics of your business and team. Practicing Agile at an enterprise level is great. But creating a culture of Agile invites lasting and sustainable change.

## Chapter 29

# Conclusion

I am not perfect in Agile or Scrum. I am not even close to it. What is great about being in this position is the fact that I have to keep learning and keep trying to improve. *The process of learning is my greatest asset and tool*. Through working for some of the biggest and most successful Fortune 500 companies, startups, government agencies, private companies, and nonprofits, I have had the opportunity to see product development from so many different angles. I've seen the good and the bad, the pretty and the ugly. I've seen teams grow and flourish and teams rise and fall implementing Agile frameworks and tools. I've been a part of the failure to implement Agile, and I've also even held the responsibility for failing to implement Agile. Thankfully, I've

**159**

also been at the top, implementing Agile successfully and being the premier driver for the continued success in a business. Those are the moments in which I delight. Those are the moments that make all the hard work worthwhile. Those are the moments when I've turned lessons from failure into linchpins for success. I'm still growing, I'm still learning, and I don't quite have it perfect yet. Frankly, I don't believe I'll ever have it perfect. What I do know, though, is that continually educating oneself and striving for greatness will find its reward in the process. The process of learning is where all the fun begins and ends.

# *Index*

*Index*